EVERY STUDENT'S GUIDE TO THE INTERNET

WINDOWS VERSION

McGraw-Hill

New York   St. Louis
San Francisco   Auckland
Bogotá   Carcas   Lisbon
London   Madrid
Mexico   Milan
Montreal   New Delhi
Paris   San Juan
Singapore   Sydney
Tokyo   Toronto

KEIKO PITTER

SARA AMATO

JOHN CALLAHAN

NIGEL KERR

ERIC TILTON

ROBERT MINATO

THE McGRAW-HILL COMPANIES, INC.
San Francisco, CA 94133

Every Student's Guide to the Internet: Windows Version

3 4 5 6 7 8 9 0   F G R F G R   9 0 9 8 7 6

ISBN 0-07-052107-7

Sponsoring editor: Frank Ruggirello
Editorial assistant: Kyle Thomes
Production supervisor: Natalie Durbin
Project manager: Cecelia G. Morales
Copyeditor: Ryan Stuart
Cover designer: Janet Bollow
Compositor: Arizona Publication Service
Printer and binder: Quebecor Printing Fairfield, Inc.

Library of Congress Card Catalog No. 95-77457

CONTENTS

CHAPTER 4   GOPHER AND VERONICA: WHAT'S ON THE MENU?   65

CHAPTER 7   WAIS: INDEXES AND DATABASES   133

CHAPTER 8   WORLD WIDE WEB (NETSCAPE): BRINGING IT ALL TOGETHER   153

PREFACE

TO THE STUDENT

The Internet, one of today's most powerful communication and information resources, gives millions of people around the world access to current and archived information on a multitude of topics. The Internet can be a tremendous help to you in your studies now and later in life. By following the easy-to-use instructions, *Every Student's Guide to the Internet: Windows Version* will enable you to search the world efficiently for information and communicate with individuals of widely divergent backgrounds.

While learning how to access the Internet, you will also learn the underlying concepts and strategies involved. Various Internet tools are discussed, along with the types of communication and information you can retrieve using those tools. This text takes full advantage of the Windows graphical user interface, however, the skills you learn will allow you to feel comfortable in any platform (Macintosh, UNIX, or Windows) or environment (a library index or a database at a research institute). You will find these skills invaluable in the constantly shifting landscape of the Internet.

TO THE INSTRUCTOR

Every Student's Guide to the Internet: Windows Version is written specifically for college and high school students, no matter what their field of study. This book can be used for short courses or training workshops on the Internet or as a supplement to courses in introductory computing, freshman orientation, and so on.

The book is organized so it can be used for teaching in the classroom or as a self-paced course. Each chapter begins with a list of objectives and ends with a chapter summary, a list of key terms, review questions, online exercises, and discussion topics. A series of projects, a list of useful Internet resources, a further reading list, and a glossary of key terms are found at the end of the book.

An Instructor's Manual, free to adopters, is also available. This manual includes teaching tips, answers to review questions and exercises, additional exercises, and projects not in the text.

Whenever possible, educational examples are used so students can relate concepts easily to their immediate environment. We hope to instill in readers a sense of excitement about the Internet, as well as give them the ability to use it effectively.

This book offers the following benefits.

✦ Simply written with the beginner in mind, it teaches students how to access various types of information and provides strategies for finding and using resources.

✦ It provides access to online resources at Willamette University created specifically for use with the book: an e-mail address to which students can send messages for practice and a listserv discussion group called esgti-l to which students can subscribe for practice using the listserv and for discussing topics with other students using the book. Students can subscribe by sending the following message to listproc@willamette.edu:

subscribe esgti-l <*full name*>

A confirmation and instruction on how to use the listserv will be sent.

✦ It also provides Internet online support. Students can receive help by sending a message to the listserv esgti-l or by contacting any of the authors via e-mail. Their e-mail addresses are as follows:

Keiko Pitter	kpitter@willamette.edu
Sara Amato	samato@cwu.edu
John Callahan	jcallaha@willamette.edu
Nigel Kerr	nigel@umich.edu
Robert Minato	rminato@willamette.edu
Eric Tilton	jtilton@willamette.edu

✦ It keeps users informed of the Internet updates and changes that are pertinent to use of the book via a Web page maintained by authors. The URL is http://www.willamette.edu/~kpitter/esgti.html.

OUR STRATEGY

The greatest challenge in writing a book like this is the dynamic nature of the Internet. Available resources and the popularity of tools on the Internet change daily. We therefore believe it is important to teach the basic concepts behind each tool so students can adapt to any platform and any tool that will be available in the future. At the same time, we set up a relatively stable environment through the computing facility at Willamette University that students can access both for practice now and for use in the future.

We assume readers have minimal technical experience. However, we also assume that the user is familiar with the use of a PC and Windows, understands Windows terminology, and knows how to operate a mouse or use the keyboard to make a selection onscreen. The reader must also have an account on an Internet host computer.

The PC in use must be on a network with an Internet host computer and have copies of the following client software installed: Eudora for Windows, WSGopher, Uwterm, WS_FTP, WinVN, WinWAIS, and Netscape. Undoubtedly, you will be using more current versions of software than the ones used for examples in this book. The versions used here are Eudora for Windows 1.4 , WSGopher 1.2, Uwterm 0.97i, WS_FTP 95.01.11, WinVN 0.93.11, WinWAIS 2.4, and Netscape 1.1N. Information on how to obtain these software packages is given in the Internet Resources and Directories section at the back of the book. Also, the Instructor's Guide gives some help on installation.

ACKNOWLEDGMENTS

We wish to thank Daris Howard of Ricks College and Michael Harris of Del Mar College for their input, and countless users of our UNIX and Macintosh books for sending us constructive messages, many of which came through the listserv esgti-l. We also want to thank the students and staff of the Willamette University for their support and Frank Ruggirello of McGraw-Hill for hanging in there.

INTERNET OR BUST

Imagine that you are visiting a very large, vibrant city. From the apartment where you are staying, you see buildings, streets, avenues, districts, and boroughs, stretching as far as the eye can see. Imagine leaving the building and entering the heart of the city. You find a bewildering array of shops, stores, museums, libraries, schools, houses, businesses of all kinds, dance clubs, restaurants, and more! You can take nearly any kind of transport to get around town: You can hire a taxi, take the bus, descend to the subways, ride a bicycle, or even walk. The people are diverse as well, even more varied than the places and things to do here. Some of them you would like to meet; others, not. The things you can do here are many and varied, and with time and energy, you can see a lot in one day. From morning till night, there is always something to do, something to see. And you will probably never see all of it, no matter how long you're here, because it's always changing.

Now imagine that the only way to get to that "city" is through your computer. Imagine a "place," countless uncharted "places," where people meet and interact, where information passes back and forth, where all kinds of activities—scholarly, business, intellectual, and just plain fun—take place. Imagine being able to sit at your computer, seeing this virtual metropolis through your computer screen, moving back and forth by telling the computer where you want to go. There is nowhere you can't go in this vast, ethereal place, and yet you never leave the room.

This place is the Internet.

OBJECTIVES

Upon completing the material presented in this chapter, you should understand the following aspects of the Internet:

✦ The concept behind the Internet

✦ Terminology used when dealing with the Internet

✦ The domain names

✦ Available Internet resources

✦ Tools for using the Internet

✦ Guidelines for behavior on the Internet

PROLOGUE

Here you are—a new student. The person working at the registration desk says, "You probably want to get an e-mail account right away, right? Your history professor is really hooked on **the 'net**.[1] He requires everyone in his class to use it for all sorts of things." You smile and walk away, unsure of yourself. What exactly did "all sorts of things" mean?

You wander over to the computer lab. A group of students is huddled around a couple of computers, all staring at one screen. You get curious. They are looking at some really nifty color images on the screen. They're gabbing about something called "Genetic Art" that they're looking at from "over in Pittsburgh, over at Carnegie Mellon." You get the feeling that they are using the Internet.

You've heard of the Internet and the Information Superhighway. Who hasn't? It's on the news everywhere. You really need to learn to use this thing. From the sound of it, you need to learn to use it right away. But where do you start? What do you have to know? How is the Internet going to help you as a student?

WHAT IS THE INTERNET?

The Internet is often referred to as the network of networks—a communication medium made possible by computers and networks. People exchange all kinds of information, in innumerable social contexts, on the Internet. Research and information pass back and forth ceaselessly. It is a fluid and dynamic environment; it has no definite boundaries, its limitations imposed only by available software and

---

[1]   *The 'net* is a term used by many to refer to the Internet.

hardware technology. It has been used exhaustively by the scientific and academic communities for many years. With the recent surge in interest by business and government, the Internet or its successor computer network will be of major importance to tomorrow's world. As a citizen of tomorrow, you need to learn how to use the tools for exploring the 'net, its information, and the people on it.

HOW WILL THE INTERNET HELP ME?

The Internet stretches from New England to New Zealand, with points of access at thousands of colleges and companies around the world. Using it, you can send a message to a friend across the ocean, obtain free (or cheap) software, and discuss world issues with the world. A large number of those who use the Internet are college students, and it can be a handy way to get in touch with friends and professors, both locally and from afar. You most likely have access to this global, instant connection through your school, now.

In description, the Internet sometimes seems a little bit of a pale thing. The question often asked is, "But what can it do?" This question may never be satisfactorily answered—at least, not in a way that would satisfy those who would swear by the Internet. In simplest terms, it can do this: It can send information from one computer to another. The trick is that the computers involved can, and often do, span the world. Imagine, if you will, taking the senior thesis you have just completed, sending it to your professor (who is on sabbatical in Germany), and having it arrive in a matter of seconds. Or sharing real-time scientific data between two experiments being performed, respectively, in Tokyo and Paris—or Dallas and Moscow—or Salem and London. Or browsing through online art galleries and exhibits at the Smithsonian from a classroom in a rural community.

You will encounter two kinds of things on the Internet: people and information. Both can help you as you progress in your academic career.

People. The Internet allows you to be in contact with people—a lot of people. There are tools, such as newsgroups and electronic mail, that can assist you in communicating with other people, people who are interested in the same topics that you are. These people are often more than eager to help out, providing answers to questions and engaging you in thoughtful discussions.

Information. The Internet is a medium for accessing a vast amount of information. A number of tools for information retrieval are discussed in this book. You can use these tools to find reference materials on the Internet, such as:

◆ Growing collections of electronic books, from *Alice in Wonderland* to *Hacker Crackdown.*

- ✦ Economic and social statistical data, such as census information, daily exchange rates, and government budgets and reports.
- ✦ Fine arts and music, including digital images of art.
- ✦ Historical information, including several online exhibits from the Library of Congress and the Smithsonian.

It should be mentioned, however, that while the Internet is a wonderful resource, it's not perfect. For one thing, you can't find information on everything by using the Internet. However, you can often find out about useful alternate and supplementary sources of information not on the Internet, in addition to what you might find at your library or learn about from your professors. For another thing, you should be concerned with the reliability of information you find on the Internet. Most of the information available online has been supplied by volunteers, and while you can often trust it, it can also occasionally contain inaccurate and misleading information. You should always be circumspect with information found online; be sure to double-check all facts before citing them.

BIRTH OF A NETWORK

The evolution of the Internet and network access in general has been similar to the development of any other useful resource. Since its genesis in early networks, tools and utilities have been developed to make access easier and more flexible. This development continues today. It is important to understand why the Internet came about in the first place, for this history helps explain the allure of computer-mediated communication today.

Our history begins in the 1960s when scientists and researchers both inside and outside of academia were confronted with a problem in communication. In those days, it was rather time-consuming and laborious to share research information around the country; the vital centers of research were often far apart, and it was difficult to share ideas and data. For scientific research to continue and grow unhampered by geographic constraints, scientists needed a new, rapid, and dependable method of communication.

Computers were seen as a logical solution. Text was a flexible communication medium, and a computer could process and store text quite nicely, even print it out on paper if desired. If one computer could speak to another computer, text could be sent from computer to computer. The problem lay in getting all the different computers in the country to talk to one another. At that time, there were many different kinds of computers, not all of them compatible, even at the same university or site! Different kinds of computers stored and processed information in slightly different formats, which meant that some kind of translation scheme was necessary for one computer to talk to another. And if more than two

BOX 1.1

QUICK PREVIEW OF THE WEB

One reason for the increased interest in and popularity of the Internet is the powerful software tool called the World Wide Web, or the Web. The Web wipes out some of the technical and geographic hurdles that have been limiting most users from using the 'net for anything more than electronic mail. The Web also makes it easy for anyone to publish information that others can use.

To access information on the Web, you need to use a Web browser program, of which there are many to choose from. The most popular product today is Netscape, whch is covered in Chapter 8. A year ago, the most popular browser was Mosaic, and there will be several more browsers introduced in the coming year. They all employ the same concept—hypertext.

In an onscreen display, certain words are underlined, or a button may appear. When you select or click underlined words or buttons, a new display appears. The display may even be multimedia, meaning that it may include graphics, motion video, and sound. However, the extent of what you can view or hear will depend on the Web browser being used and the type of computer you are using. If you access the Internet from home, the type of connection and the speed of the modem you use will also affect how effectively you can browse the Web. Eventually, access to the Web will become an integral part of computer usage at home, school, and business.

It is tempting, therefore, to think that all you need to learn to use the Internet is to learn how to use a Web browser. This is becoming more and more true, but it is not completely true yet; you must not limit your knowledge of the Internet to the Web alone.

For a quick preview of the Web, just do the following:

 Look at the Program Manager window for the following Netscape icon, then double-click on it.

N

From the File menu, select Open Location or press CTRL-**L**.

In the Open Location text box, type **www.whitehouse.gov** and click on Open. If you do not see graphics, click on the Images button found just under the menu.

You are now looking at the electronic information provided by the White House. To search this information space, you must be very intuitive—various words will be highlighted and underlined, and you can click on those words to find out more about specific information. As mentioned, you will learn more about navigating through Web documents like this in Chapter 8.

 When you are done, open the File menu and select Exit.

or three types of computers were involved, this translation could get very complicated very quickly.

The solution that arose was to have a network standard for communication. The computers would be connected to one or more other computers through physical cables in a giant network across the country. Any text or data put on the network would be translated, or *encoded,* into a standard format. Information received by a computer would be translated back, or *decoded,* to its own format. This allowed anyone with a computer having an encoding and decoding program to connect to this network. This network came to fruition in 1969, with the first system at UCLA; many more followed. This first network, a Department of Defense project known as the ARPANET, was not the Internet as we know it today. The original ARPANET method of connecting computers was eventually phased out, but it laid the foundation for what eventually became the Internet. What we now know as the Internet arose in the 1980s, with the creation of a standard method of connecting computer networks, and with the National Science Foundation's creation of the NSFNet linking supercomputing centers together.

BOX 1.2	TCP/IP

Although most people say that the standard for the Internet is TCP/IP, the "IP" (Internet Protocol) is the important part. The purpose of the Internet Protocol is to deliver a piece of information (called a *datagram*) from one machine to another by moving it from one network to another. Every machine on the Internet is identified by a unique IP address. For humans, the address is usually displayed as four numbers separated by dots (for example, 145.12.3.19). Part of the IP address specifies the network that the machine is on and part specifies an individual machine on that network.

The Internet is a network of networks. The networks it connects are themselves networks of networks. It may continue for several levels! Typically, your university or college has some form of campus computer network. The campus network may be connected to a regional network, which serves a geographic or logical area. The regional network is usually connected to a larger network, which might cover an entire country. This larger network is then connected to other large networks.

When a machine on your campus network needs to send an IP datagram to a machine outside its local network, it uses a special machine on its network called a *router.* A router is connected to more than one network, and is able to pass a datagram from one network to another. It is not uncommon for an IP datagram to be handled by 15 routers before it gets to the network (and the machine) for which it was destined!

The standard established on the Internet is called **TCP/IP**. Any computer that connects to the Internet must support TCP/IP. The Internet is composed of many separate networks which all use TCP/IP. When one network is connected to another, a device called a **router** connects to both networks and passes information between the two networks.

THE DOMAIN NAME SYSTEM

When a site wishes to start a TCP/IP network, it is assigned a unique range of addresses. The site will use one address for each device on the network. The range of addresses could be large or small depending on the number of devices the site has or anticipates having. Whenever someone wants to access a computer on the site, the person must specify the address of the computer. If someone wants to send e-mail to a user at a site, the sender must specify the user name of the recipient, along with the address of the computer on which the recipient has an account.

To the devices on the network, each address is a number, called an **Internet Protocol (IP) address**. An IP address is usually displayed as a series of four numbers separated by periods. For example, "158.104.1.1" is the IP address of a computer at Willamette University. However, since many people have a hard time remembering numbers, especially large ones, there is usually a name associated with each address. In the early days, names and addresses were listed in a file that was passed around the network, but as the number of machines increased, so did the size of the file. Every time a new machine was added to the network the file became out-of-date, and would have to be updated and copied around again!

In the modern Internet, a site usually requests a name, called a **domain name**, along with its range of addresses. The site is responsible for any names "under" that domain and for entering in the corresponding address for each name. Domain names are a series of words separated by periods. Willamette University has the domain name willamette.edu, so all machines "under" that domain are managed and named by Willamette University. For example, jupiter.willamette.edu is the name for the address 158.104.1.1 mentioned earlier.

| **NOTE:** | In the IP address and domain names, a period (.) is referred to as a "dot." |

When you use the domain name in accessing a computer on the Internet, the domain name is translated by the Domain Name System into the host's corresponding IP address. In the domain name michael.ai.mit.edu, for example, the Internet host michael is in the domain called ai, which is in the domain mit.

That is an educational institution (indicated by edu). In other words, a domain name contains information about the computer system.

Just as mail addresses are subdivided into countries containing smaller units, such as states and cities, domain names are divided into various level domains. The last word in the domain name is the **top-level domain**. The top-level domain can be either the geographical location or the countries and territories in which the host computer is located. They include the following:

AQ	Antartica	FR	France	NZ	New Zealand
AR	Argentina	GR	Greece	PR	Puerto Rico
AT	Austria	HK	Hong Kong	PT	Portugal
AU	Australia	HU	Hungary	SE	Sweden
BE	Belgium	IE	Ireland	SG	Singapore
BR	Brazil	IL	Israel	TN	Tunisia
CA	Canada	IN	India	TW	Taiwan
CH	Switzerland	IT	Italy	UK	United Kingdom
CL	Chile	JP	Japan	US	United States
DE	Germany	KR	Korea	VE	Venezuela
DK	Denmark	MX	Mexico	ZA	South Africa
ES	Spain	NL	The Netherlands		
FI	Finland	NO	Norway		

If a geographic location is not specified, it is assumed to be the United States. In fact, within the United States, most network sites use the "organizational" identification for the top-level domain instead.

COM	Commercial organizations
EDU	Educational and research institutions
GOV	Government agencies
MIL	Military agencies
NET	Major network support centers
ORG	Other organizations
INT	International organizations

The second-to-last word gives a descriptive (or nondescriptive!) reference to the organization: you might expect stjude.edu to refer to an educational institution by the name of St. Jude's, nwnet.net to be a NWNet network service provider, and apple.com to be company called Apple. All other words in the domain name are subdomains within the domain—that is, subdivisions within the organization. For example, jupiter.willamette.edu and mercury.willamette.edu are both computers within the Willamette University network.

THE CLIENT/SERVER MODEL

Most of the programs described in this book utilize the **client/server model**. This model allows for a special relationship between the computer you are using—a PC running Microsoft Windows in this book—and the (possibly remote) computer than has information you seek. Each of these programs has two parts: the client part and the server part.

The client program runs on the computer you are using, such as your PC. It facilitates information access by doing the behind-the-scenes work of opening connections to distant computers, sending your requests, and receiving and displaying results.

The server software runs on the computers that provide the information. A server is usually a powerful computer capable of handling information requests from many clients simultaneously.

When a tool follows the client/server model, two things are implied about its function and dependability. The first is that unless you are using a computer that is installed with a client software, you cannot access the server. The second is that a client depends on a server being available to provide information. If the server computer is inoperative, for example, a client cannot access information. If a server is under a heavy load of many client requests, its response will be very slow.

For most tools, you can get a version of client software to run on almost any **platform**, which refers to the kind of hardware and operating system used by the computer. **UNIX** is a platform. A personal computer running under MS-DOS is a platform. One that utilizes Microsoft Windows is a different platform. The Macintosh is yet another platform.

The platform that you use influences what your client software will be like. Macintosh and Windows clients will have the same kind of "friendly" user interface that you are used to from other Macintosh and Windows software products. That is, the user interface will be very visual, commands will be available on a menu bar, and information will appear in windows and dialog boxes on the screen. UNIX clients will have the flavor of UNIX machines: The display is text-based, commands are typed at a prompt, and there is generally only one thing onscreen at a time. It is not fair to say that one platform and its clients are inherently better than another; each has its own capabilities and drawbacks. What you use at your site will depend on such factors as availability, cost, and the preferences of administrators at your site.

Although this book is written for the PC running Windows, nearly all of the tools described here have counterparts on the UNIX and Macintosh platforms, and the lessons in this book will apply to the programs available on these other platforms. While the specifics of how a command is given may vary, the strategies involved in finding information will not change.

BOX 1.3 | **CLIENTS FOR PERSONAL COMPUTERS ARE INDEED PERSONAL**

Client software programs for personal computers are quite nice. A Macintosh or Windows client lets you use the same kind of user interface—such as mouse and icons—to select commands. Most likely, commands found in the Windows File menu will be there. Print, Save, and Quit will do the same task you expect them to do.

These clients often are written for a "personal" computer environment, however. They often assume that one user uses that computer. For example, an e-mail program will go ahead and automatically insert your name and e-mail address as that of the sender, or retrieve all your incoming mail and put it on the hard drive of your computer.

While this can be a very convenient feature, it does not work too well in a multiuser environment.

TOOLS OF THE INTERNET: WHAT DO YOU NEED?

The three basic tools for using the Internet are electronic-mail (e-mail), Telnet, and File Transfer Protocol (FTP).

- ✦ **E-mail** allows users to send messages to each other.
- ✦ **Telnet** allows users to connect, or login, to any computer on the Internet.
- ✦ **FTP** allows a user to connect to a remote computer solely for the purpose of transferring files: uploading (sending to the remote machine) or downloading (getting back from the remote machine) files and data.

Other tools were developed to extend this basic functionality:

- ✦ **Listserv**, short for "mailing list server," allows a group of people with common interests to send messages to each other. It requires that interested people subscribe to a discussion group, which is essentially a mailing list. When a subscriber sends a message to listserv, the message is sent to all other subscribers.
- ✦ **Usenet** is another discussion forum for people interested in a topic. There is no master list of subscribers for each topic; rather, there are many sites that provide users with access to the thousands of discussion groups. Anyone with access to Usenet may use a news reader program to post and read articles from the group.
- ✦ **Archie**, short for Archive, was created to query FTP sites for their contents and make that information available to users. A user can search Archie for files by giving Archie the title (or partial title) of the files being searched for.

Using the results of an Archie search, the user can determine which FTP site has the desired files, then use FTP to download them.

✦ Another tool that helps you locate information is the **WAIS (Wide Area Information Server)** index. WAIS indexes are a popular way to index any large body of electronic information (documents, data files, images, and so forth). Information can be searched for by using keywords.

✦ **Gopher**, **Hytelnet**, and the **World Wide Web (WWW)** attempt to bind together the various tools used on the Internet to give the user a simple, consistent interface to a wide variety of information. The user sees only a menu or document that gives access to further menus of options and documents. Fortunately for the average Internet user, many people work very hard to create useful menus and documents to help the budding infonaut find the information he or she seeks.

Each of these tools allows access to the information on the Internet. No one tool is suited to delivering all kinds of information, so you have to learn how to use most (if not all) of them. You also need to know in which situations one tool is more useful than another.

If you are trying to communicate directly with other people, either specific users or people with similar academic or research interests, e-mail, listservs, and Usenet are the most direct and effective tools. If you do not know any specific people yet, you can use the forums that listservs and Usenet provide as places to look for people interested in the things that intrigue you.

If you're trying to access specific data out of a large body, such as books in library collections, specific documents or papers out of a collection, a specific user's e-mail address, particular articles, or statistical data of some kind, you are more likely to encounter these using the tools Telnet, FTP, Archie, and WAIS.

If you are new to the Internet and need to get up to speed quickly so that you can make use of the resources on the Internet, Gopher and the WWW are your tools.

WARNINGS

One characteristic of the Internet is its extreme volatility. Computers make it astoundingly easy to move data, change interfaces, and set up and take down services, and you will find that these things happen frequently. In a library, you can be reasonably assured that the same books, periodicals, and reference works will be there for weeks and months, but the status of services and tools on the Internet is in constant flux. A Gopher you used last week may mysteriously vanish without warning this week; a WAIS index that never seemed very useful may get a sudden infusion of information. Options offered on a menu change, and so on. There is no way to tell what the future will bring for resources on the Internet. Only rarely (such as with government servers) is the presence of a resource mandated; even then it is subject to radical change. Most often the information is supplied and maintained by volunteers, so the quality and timeliness of it will depend heavily on the dedication of that volunteer.

When using this book and the Internet, you should be mindful of this potential for rapid change. You may find the screen actually displayed to be radically different from what is shown in this book, or you may find a resource referenced here to be nonexistent.

You need to adapt to changes and be able to take alternative actions. If one site is not available for use, then use another, similar computer site. If a menu option no longer exists, look around to see what you can use instead. You must be patient and willing to make the fluidity of the Internet work for you, instead of being paralyzed by constant change.

To that end, this book presents strategies for Internet navigation. Rather than concentrating on specific sites, we'll talk about the indexes of information that can lead you to the information you seek. Rather than giving you addresses for every topic under the sun, we'll give you pointers to help you discover everything under the sun and keep up with the Internet's changes.

THE PRESENT

Millions of users from varied backgrounds around the world use the Internet every day. This is a considerable change from 20 years ago, when access was limited to researchers in the sciences—computer science in particular. The communication potential of the Internet is now available to a wider group of people, who bring a wider range of uses for the Internet. These uses all center around communication and access to information, but the subject matter varies dramatically.

It is not surprising that this migration of broader academic research and culture onto the 'net has attracted attention around the world. The Internet, and networks in general, are very useful for all kinds of communication. Civic and social organizations, business, and government have all expressed interest in promoting and establishing networks for general use.

In the United States, this effort is focused on the National Information Infrastructure put forth by the Clinton Administration. Telecommunications companies, cable companies, and the accompanying computer industries are all eager to create the market for networked information. Networks will figure in more

BOX 1.4

WHY ARE THERE SO MANY UNIX COMPUTERS?

We've already mentioned that there were many different platforms in use in the 1960s. In the early 1970s, with the advent of a mainframe operating system (the program that coordinates and manages all the computer's functions) called UNIX, this began to change. UNIX was distributed by AT&T *free* to colleges and universities, because AT&T itself was forbidden to sell software by the federal government (a potential violation of antitrust laws). Because it was free, many institutions and their computing managers tried it. It was found to be a powerful and extendable operating system, one for which it was relatively easy to develop programs and applications. It caught on around the United States and the world, and is today, in various forms, one of the most popular computer operating systems for mainframes, supercomputers, and even some powerful desktop machines and workstations. UNIX was also very *portable*, or able to be used on a variety of different physical machines; with some changes in the software, UNIX could run on many different computers. UNIX and a very few other popular operating systems indirectly encouraged standards on the 'net. Programs for network transmission and reception could be written and ported to other UNIX systems with relative ease. The programmer and user could both enjoy some stability and consistency across many computers.

This stability has continued to the present day, with IBM-compatibles and Macintosh computers dominating the market for desktop computers. Both of these platforms are stable and standardized enough for a few basic programs and software to allow them to communicate over local and wide-area networks of computers, to mainframes, and to other personal computers. What you can accomplish on one computer, you can pretty much accomplish on any other computer of its power and magnitude. The important idea here is that different kinds of computers do not restrict networking: Tools can be written for compatibility.

areas of life for more people around the world, from entertainment applications to work and research.

This makes it even more important to be familiar with computer-mediated communication and research. Networks will begin to creep up in all areas of life, quite apart from the Internet itself. Strategies for effective use of Internet resources will transfer to effective use of electronic and computer resources in general. Consider the pervasiveness of the telephone—and imagine your telephone replaced by a computer screen in 20 years.

NETIQUETTE

Even if the idea of the Internet is a bit vague in your mind at the moment, you can proceed with exploring it; you will form clearer impressions as you learn to use the various tools. What is vitally important to understand before embarking is that the Internet is really about people. When you venture onto the Internet, you are sharing a large, yet finite, space with hundreds of thousands of other people. You will communicate with some of them through e-mail and other direct methods, you will hear about many others indirectly (as well as be heard about!), and you will encounter still others only in the sense that you are both trying to use the same resource at the same time, or that they are managing computers that you are trying to use.

In this sense, being on the Internet is like being in any other social situation. Good behavior and respect for others is important. Riding on a bus, eating lunch at a restaurant, and attending a concert all have guidelines and rules for behavior, and the Internet is no different. The norms and rules are there so that everyone has the chance to enjoy the Internet. It is difficult to get a firm grip on what these norms are, however, because the Internet is such a large and fluid place. There are policies laid down by local and wide-area network administrators. There are rules set by the keepers of various resources on how they are to be used. There are rules set by moderators of discussion forums to determine what is acceptable in that forum. These rules will change wherever you go, and it may be difficult to determine what they are.

If you don't know what the rules are, or they are not explicitly stated, a very simple guideline for Internet behavior is as follows: What are the possible consequences of your actions for other users? Is it possible for someone to be disturbed or hurt by what you send to them, and is it possible that computing resources may be hindered or crash because of your activities? If someone else, another user or administrator, will have to expend extra effort because of things you've written or done, then writing or doing them is probably not a good idea. Is there a better way to express your thoughts, a more appropriate time to attempt to use resources, a better way to use them? Because accessing the Internet is so immediate, it is easy to get carried away by rash thoughts and emotions. This generally leads to trouble and bad feelings. The primary goal of the Internet is communication; it's best to use the 'net to talk with others and come to amicable solutions to problems you encounter. Good behavior reflects well on you as a user, and you'll find that it makes you a lot of friends on the Internet.

Look before you leap. Think before you speak.

Try to remember this at all times, both in making decisions and in judging other users' behavior. Making the effort to communicate with other people, rather than simply talking at them, will make your Internet experience much more pleasant and productive. With this in mind, you're ready to step out on the Internet.

SUMMARY

In this chapter, many of the terms and concepts that are necessary to use the Internet are introduced:

✦ The Internet is composed of networks and computers supporting a common data transmission standard called TCP/IP.

✦ The computers on the Internet are given an address, which is a unique IP address and an equivalent domain name. An IP address is a series of four numbers connected by dots, while a domain name is a series of words separated by dots. The last word in the domain name gives the geographical location or the organization type that runs the host computer.

✦ The Internet contains a variety of tools and resources that can be used for communication, data archiving and retrieval, discussion groups, and so on.

✦ The Internet is in constant flux, and it pays to keep abreast of changes so that you can continue to use the 'net even if your sources change.

✦ It is important to be respectful of other users on the Internet, to allow everyone the opportunity to enjoy the communication and resources. Solutions to problems almost always exist.

KEY TERMS

Archie	Internet Protocol	The Internet
client/server model	(IP) address	top-level domain
domain name	listserv	UNIX
e-mail	platform	Usenet
File Transfer Protocol	router	WAIS (Wide Area
(FTP)	TCP/IP	Information Server)
Gopher	Telnet	World Wide Web
Hytelnet	The 'net	(WWW)

REVIEW QUESTIONS

1. What is the Internet?

2. What type of resources can you find on the Internet?

3. What does the Department of Defense have to do with the Internet?

4. What purpose does a router serve?

5. What's the relationship between an IP address and a domain name?

6. What does top-level domain indicate? Give some examples with meanings.

7. What is a client/server model?

8. What is a platform? What does it mean when someone refers to a "client for a particular platform"?

9. Describe three basic tools for utilizing the Internet.

10. How stable are the resources and services on the Internet? Explain.

DISCUSSION QUESTIONS

1. From the brief overview presented in the chapter, how could using the Internet change your daily life and your academic pursuits? What impact could this have on students and faculty in general?

2. If there weren't an Internet or any kind of computer network connecting educational institutions, how could your academic experience change? What would be the impact on academics in general?

3. Which of the Internet tools outlined in the chapter interests you the most? Why?

4. What kinds of information would you like to find on the Internet? Keep these things in mind as you move through the book. You may just run across them!

E-MAIL/LISTSERV

CHAPTER 2

OBJECTIVES

Upon completing the material presented in this chapter, you should understand the following aspects of the Internet:

- ✦ The concept behind e-mail
- ✦ How to use e-mail software
- ✦ How to create and send an e-mail message
- ✦ How to read and save an e-mail message
- ✦ How to reply to or forward an e-mail message
- ✦ Effective use of e-mail
- ✦ The concept behind a listserv
- ✦ How to subscribe to a listserv list
- ✦ Listserv etiquette
- ✦ How to locate interesting listservs

BEFORE YOU START

In order to perform online exercises in this chapter, you need the following:

- ✦ An account on a UNIX computer connected to the Internet, with a Post Office Protocol version 3 (POP3) server

✦ An IBM PC compatible running Windows and connected to the Internet

✦ A copy of Eudora for Windows installed on the PC you are using. The version used here is 1.4.

WHAT IS ELECTRONIC MAIL?

Electronic mail (e-mail) is a system for sending messages or files to the accounts of other computer users. The sender and recipient(s) may be on the same or on a different computer. Electronic mail works very much like regular postal mail. Every user on the network has a private mailbox. Once received, your mail is kept for you until you decide to discard it. Like regular postal mail, you must know a user's address to send a message. If the mail system cannot deliver your message, it will make every attempt to return it to you, but it is possible for misaddressed messages to get lost somewhere along the way.

E-mail can be used not only to exchange correspondence with friends, but to transfer documents, obtain electronic copies of books, subscribe to electronic news services or to journals, and to obtain just about anything that is stored on a computer. You can even search databases using e-mail. E-mail is the primary communication tool used on the Internet. In fact, many users are unaware that there are other services on the Internet.

As a student, you can use e-mail to keep in touch with classmates or friends who attend other colleges. If your parents have access to e-mail, it's a good way to keep in touch. Additionally, you can subscribe to various discussion groups and electronic journals, as will be explained later in this chapter.

HOW DOES IT WORK?

To send a message by e-mail, you need to know the recipient's address and how to compose and send the message using mail software. To read e-mail, you need to know how to read the message using mail software. You will also want to know how to archive (save), delete, and reply to messages you receive.

NOTE: Although it is possible to attach different kinds of files (such as word processing or spreadsheet files) to your e-mail, you will cause confusion unless the recipient uses the same e-mail software as you do or knows what to do with the attached file. For the most part, it is safest to send or attach **plain text files** (also called **ASCII files**) only. Text or ASCII files can be read by any computer.

E-MAIL SOFTWARE

When you write and read e-mail, you use an e-mail program—one that will run on your desktop or host computer. Most computer systems offer one or more e-mail programs from which to choose. All e-mail software will let you compose and send e-mail, then read and organize the e-mail you receive. Your choice of e-mail will depend on how you're accessing the Internet and what is available to you. The program described here is Eudora for Windows, version 1.4. Eudora is

BOX 2.1	**POP MAIL SERVERS**

Consider the following problem: You and the other 100 people in your dorm each have a network connection in your room. Each of you has a PC running Windows, and all of the PCs are connected to the Internet, so you can use all of the Internet tools discussed in this book.

But what happens when someone tries to send you mail? If they tried to send the mail directly to your PC, there are several potential problems. First, they'd have to know the name of your machine: Would your address be jmullen@room206.metanoia-hall.unseen.edu or just jmullen@futon.unseen.edu? And what if your machine is turned off when they try to send you mail? For these reasons and more, you need something called a Post Office Protocol (POP) mail server.

The POP mail server is installed on a centralized machine on campus. This machine is always on, and it provides the same address (unseen.edu, perhaps) for everyone. Whenever anyone tries to send you mail, it goes to this machine and stays there. Then, when you are ready to check your e-mail on your own machine, your PC can ask the server to send you all of the mail it has received for you.

This has certain advantages, the foremost being that you can now use the familiar Microsoft Windows point-and-click interface to read and answer your e-mail. But there is one significant drawback—after the POP mail server has sent your e-mail to your machine, the e-mail messages are deleted. In other words, the only copies of your e-mail are now on your PC's hard drive.

Why is this bad? Well, as long as you read your e-mail from only one machine, this is not bad. In fact, it's pretty good, because you don't have to go across a network to retreive your e-mail. But you can't use this in a lab, for instance, because all of your e-mail will now be on the lab machine, and you can't transfer it back to the POP mail server. You have to read and delete all of it from the machine you are currently using. So, unless you have your own machine from which you always read e-mail, using POP won't be the answer for you.

a **POP mail** program; it works in conjunction with the **POP mail server** installed on the Internet host computer where you have an account. When e-mail messages are delivered to the host computer, the POP server transfers them to the Eudora program on your PC.

E-MAIL ADDRESS

As you might expect, you need a way to make sure that your e-mail gets to the right place. Just as with the postal service, you need to supply an **address** that tells your e-mail program where to deliver your letter.

Internet e-mail addresses consist of a username and a domain name separated by an at (@) sign: username@hostname.domainname. The **username** refers to the e-mail box, login name, or user ID of the recipient on that computer. For example, if a user logs into a computer as jsmith, then that is his username. The **domain name** has several parts separated by dots. The last part is an abbreviation for a geographic or administrative domain, such as au for AUstralian hosts on the Internet or edu for the EDUcational domain in the Internet. Before the geographic or administrative domain is the name of the institution or the organization. Before that is the subdomain (if it exists) within the institution, getting progressively more specific, until finally reaching the name of the individual computer, or **hostname**, on which the user account appears.

Let's say that you have a friend named Al Jones who has an account with user ID jones on the Internet host nimbus, located at University of Nevada, Reno, with domain name unr.edu. His Internet mail address would be jones@nimbus.unr.edu. Then the name might be shorter or longer. The Internet address for the user Yolanda Portofoni, with the user ID portofon, at Willamette University is "portofon@willamette.edu" since Willamette University has its system set up so that senders do not have to know on which computer user accounts reside. On

---

BOX 2.2	**IS EUDORA FREE?**

Is anything really free? Well, actually, Eudora 1.4 (and all earlier versions) *are* free. This free version works very well, and is the version described in this chapter. It can be found via FTP at ftp.qualcomm.com, in the directory /quest/windows/eudora/1.4.

On the other hand, Qualcomm makes a commercial version—versions 2.0 and greater. The commercial version has several enhancements, including MIME support (for multimedia messages), and that most important product enhancement, technical support. If you are interested in it, you can ask Qualcomm about it by e-mailing to eudora-sales@qualcomm.com.

BOX 2.3

FINDING OTHER USERS ON THE 'NET

Perhaps the best way to locate another user's e-mail address is to contact that person through a different medium and ask them directly. But this is sometimes not possible. There are a number of utilities available to locate a person's address; each method has its own quirks.

FINGER

Most UNIX hosts allow queries of their local users, a process called *fingering* that site or user. If you have an account on the local UNIX computer, you can logon and use the Finger command. To check on a specific user, the general format for UNIX machines is:

finger <*username*>@<*hostname*>

Alternatively, type:

finger @<*hostname*>

to see what users are currently logged on at that host computer.

Some host computers don't allow fingering, or permit it only during low-traffic times. If you see the message "Connection refused" or a similar message, you will need to use some method other than fingering.

FINGER FROM EUDORA

On Eudora, the Finger command is available from the <u>W</u>indows menu using the <u>P</u>h command or by pressing CTRL-**U**. You will see this dialog box:

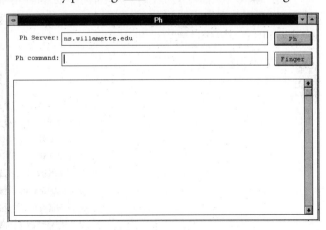

Continued on next page

BOX 2.3

FINDING OTHER USERS ON THE 'NET (*continued*)

With the insertion point in the Ph Command text box, type **<*username*>@ <*hostname*>** as instructed in the UNIX section and click on Finger to check on a specific user.

NETFIND

If you don't know a person's username, but you have a pretty good idea of what institution they might be at, you can use **Netfind**. Netfind, given a last name and the name of an organization, will search for that organization's computers and any names matching on those computers. There are many Netfind servers; only a few geographically dispersed ones are listed here. Try to use one closest to your location, and login as **netfind**. (Telnet is explained more fully in Chapter 5.)

telnet bruno.cs.colorado.edu	telnet monolith.cc.ic.ac.uk
telnet athe.wustl.edu	telnet dino.conicit.ve
telnet ds.internic.net	telnet netfind.ee.mcgill.ca
telnet netfind.anu.edu.au	telnet malloco.ing.puc.cl
telnet netfind.if.usp.br	telnet netfind.vslib.cz

CSO SERVERS

Often a university or other organization will establish a searchable index of all the people affiliated with that institution. Called a **CSO server**, these often even include employees and students who don't have e-mail addresses. The indexes also sometimes provide information such as telephone numbers and local mailing addresses. CSO servers are usually accessible through the Gopher server for that institution. If you know the name of the organization at which a person you're looking for works or studies, try using Gopher to access the Gopher server at that organization and look for a CSO server or similar searchable index. Gopher is explained in Chapter 4.

the other hand, user janet at the Chemistry Department at William and Mary College with an account on the computer called che1 may have the address janet@che1.chem.wm.edu since William and Mary College decided to create a subdomain called chem within the institution.

　　Whether or not your e-mail gets to its destination depends almost solely on whether or not the address is correct. (E-mail sometimes fails because machines or pieces of the network are unavailable, but usually the e-mail system tries to send mail for several days before giving up.)

FINDING E-MAIL ADDRESSES

The best way to find someone's e-mail address is to ask the person. There is not yet a standard way to find a person's e-mail address on the Internet. Many people now list their e-mail address along with their postal mail address on business cards and in other directories.

HOW DO I USE E-MAIL?

To use e-mail, you need to know the following: (1) how to enter the e-mail environment; (2) how to compose and send mail; (3) how to retrieve and read mail; (4) how to delete or save the received mail; (5) how to respond to mail; and finally (6) how to exit the e-mail environment. Although the commands presented here are for Eudora in the PC Windows environment, the general concepts hold for any e-mail software on any platform.

BOX 2.4

GOVERNMENTAL E-MAIL ADDRESSES

The United States government is based on representational democracy, a system requiring elected representatives to heed our collective voices. For them to do this, citizens need to let the officials know what they think. Sometimes you can reach those officials via e-mail rather than traditional "snail-mail." Here's how:

Name	Address
President	president@whitehouse.gov
Vice President	vice.president@whitehouse.gov

Some congressional members may also be accessible via e-mail. For more information, send mail to:

congress@hr.house.gov

Of course, if you don't believe in government, you can always send your requests to:

Santa Claus	santa@northpole.com

ENTERING THE E-MAIL ENVIRONMENT

 Visually locate the Eudora icon in the Program Manager window. It should look similar to the one below. If you cannot locate it, ask your instructor.

Double-click on the Eudora icon.

A dialog box appears as shown in Figure 2.1, prompting you to enter the password.

Each time you open Eudora, the program asks you to enter the password. This is the password for your user account on the host computer.

 Type in the password and click OK.

NOTE: If your password is rejected, select Check Mail from the File menu or press ⌈CTRL⌉-**M** (hold down the ⌈CTRL⌉ key and press **M**) and re-enter the password.

A progress window is momentarily displayed to inform you that an attempt is being made to reach your POP account.

If there is a problem in making connection, a dialog box similar to the one shown in Figure 2.2 is displayed.

FIGURE 2.1

FIGURE 2.2

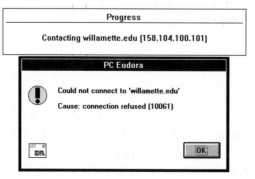

BOX 2.5

CHECKING YOUR E-MAIL IN A SHARED ENVIRONMENT

It is possible to check your e-mail in a shared computing environment, for example, in a lab, or any other place where you want to check your e-mail on a machine that's not assigned to you alone. It's not totally straightforward. There are things you need to do when you want to use Eudora in a shared environment. However, if you want to do it, you can do it as follows.

First, you need to specify yourself as the user:

Start Eudora.

Click on Cancel if you are asked for a password.

From the Special menu, select Configurations.

In the Configuration dialog box that appears, change the POP Account, Real Name, and Return Address fields as appropriate. Everything else should be fine.

POP mail will transfer mail from the POP server to the machine you are using. If you want to leave the mail on the POP server as well (just in case you want to look at it later), you need to do the following:

From the Special menu, select Switches.

In the Switches dialog box, check the Leave Mail on Server option. This prevents your e-mail from being erased from the POP server, in case you don't read it all. Also make sure Empty Trash on Quit is checked.

Now you can go ahead and check your e-mail. You can read and respond to messages and your name will be listed as that of the sender. When you are done, you want to make sure to delete all your e-mail from the machine you are using.

Exit Eudora.

To delete mail from your POP server, you'll need to log onto it occasionally and delete it from the machine itself. Ask your local computing support people for more information on how to do this.

If there is a message, the dialog box as shown in Figure 2.3 is displayed.

If you keep Eudora running in the background, it will notify you when a new message arrives for you. You can also check for new messages manually by selecting Check Mail from the File menu.

FIGURE 2.3

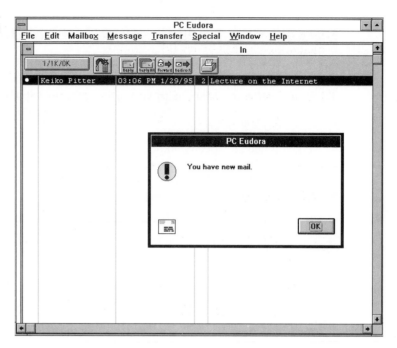

EXITING THE E-MAIL ENVIRONMENT

You will now exit Eudora.

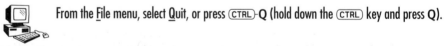 From the File menu, select Quit, or press (CTRL)-Q (hold down the (CTRL) key and press Q).

ANATOMY OF AN E-MAIL MESSAGE

An e-mail message has two parts: the header and the body. The header has information *about* the message. It gives information such as for whom the message is, who the message is from, the time the message was sent, and what the subject of the message is. It might also contain other information, such as who received a "carbon copy" (Cc:) of the message. The body, on the other hand, is the text of the message itself. You need to be aware of these two parts, because when you send e-mail you'll need to put information in both.

COMPOSING AND SENDING A MESSAGE

You will be able to practice sending an e-mail message by sending one to Yolanda Portofoni, whose e-mail address is portofon@willamette.edu. You will send a carbon copy to yourself. Yolanda will send a reply. When you receive an e-mail message, you can try other commands.

 Open Eudora by double-clicking on the Eudora icon. Enter the password as needed.

From the <u>M</u>essage menu, select <u>N</u>ew Message or press (CTRL)-**N**.

The composition window is displayed as shown in Figure 2.4 with the blinking cursor at the start of the To: field.

NOTE: This book describes only those basic features of Eudora needed to get started on using e-mail. Consult the Eudora Reference manual for the rest.

 Type **portofon@willamette.edu** in the To: field.

You will notice that your address was automatically inserted in the From field.

 Either press the (TAB) key or click the mouse to move the cursor to the Subject: field.

You need to enter an appropriate subject for the message. The subject should reflect the content of the message. Here you will use "Introduction" as the subject.

 Type **Introduction** in the Subject: field.

Similarly, enter your mail address in the Cc: (carbon copy) field.

FIGURE 2.4

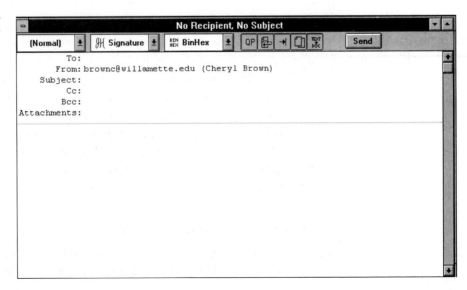

Move the cursor past the Bcc: and Attachments: fields down to the large area below the horizontal line.

You can now enter the body of the message.

 Type the body of the message. Introduce yourself to Yolanda.

The screen should look similar to the one shown in Figure 2.5.

At this point, you can either send the message or save it for later use. If you were to close the composition box by doubling-clicking on the close box on the top left corner, you would see a dialog box as shown in Figure 2.6 asking you if you want to save this message or discard it. If you decide to save it, it will be placed in the Out Box with a filled circle in front of it. The Out box is accessed by selecting Out from the Mailbox menu. See the section on saving messages later in this chapter.

 Click on the Send button.

The composition box closes and the progress window displays the transfer of the message. Eventually, the message is placed in the Out Box with "S" in front of it to indicate that it's been sent.

FIGURE 2.5

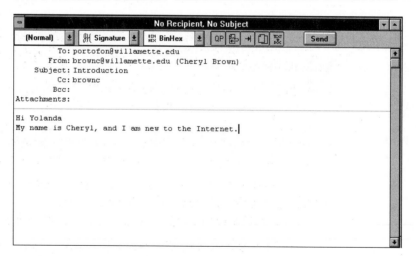

FIGURE 2.6

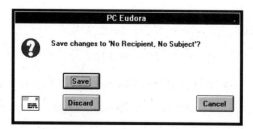

BOX 2.6		**HOW TO SEND E-MAIL TO ANOTHER NETWORK MAIL SYSTEM**

Other Network	Address on the Other Network	Internet Address
America Online	<user>	*<user>*@aol.com
AppleLink	<id>	*<id>*@applelink.apple.com
BITNET	<user>@<node>	*<user>*@*<node>*.bitnet
CompuServ	71234,567	71234.567@compuserv.com
Fidonet	JohnSmith at 1:2/3.4	john.smith@p4.f3.n2. z1.fidonet.org
MCIMail	John Smith (123-4567)	1234567@mcimail.com JSmith@mcimail.com John_Smith@mcimail.com
SprintMail	John Smith at SomeOrg	SomeOrg/G=John/S=Smth/ O=SomeOrg / ADMD=TELEMAIL/ C=US/@sprint.com

READING MESSAGES

As mentioned briefly earlier, there are two ways to spot the arrival of an e-mail message. One way is automatic; Eudora checks for mail every so many minutes as specified in the Configuration dialog box, and will notify you if there is a new message. The other is to check for mail manually by selecting Check Mail from the File menu. Right now, you will check manually.

From the File menu, select Check Mail or press (CTRL)-M. In fact, keep on doing this periodically until you do receive a reply from Yolanda Portofoni or you receive a carbon copy of the mail you sent earlier. Don't worry. You will receive a message.

When you have a message, a dialog box (as was shown in Figure 2.3) is displayed.

Click on OK.

From the Mailbox menu, select In or press (CTRL)-I.

The In mailbox window is displayed as shown in Figure 2.7, with your message summary.

To view a message, all you need to do is double-click on it in the In box display.

Double-click on the message from Yolanda or the one from yourself.

FIGURE 2.7

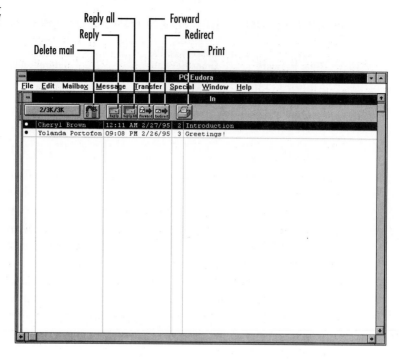

REPLYING TO A MAIL MESSAGE

To reply to a message, either highlight it on the In box summary display by click-ing on it or open it by double-clicking on it. Then, select Reply (not "Reply to") from the Message menu or press (CTRL)-**R**. You can also click on the Reply button. A new composition window is opened with the sender's address automatically in the To: field. The sender's e-mail text is also displayed in the body of the message (with an ">" in front of each line). You can edit the text as you'd like.

NOTE: You can send a reply to Yolanda. However, you may find to your dismay that—as nice an entity as Yolanda is—she is only a computer program that returns automatic replies. So any conversation with Yolanda may be a bit lackluster.

FORWARDING A MESSAGE TO ANOTHER USER

Sometimes you receive a mail message that you may wish to forward to others or include in a message of your own. To do this, either highlight the message on the In box summary display or open the message. You can then select Forward from the Message menu. A new composition window is opened with the cursor on the To: field and the original message displayed in the body of the message. You can again edit the document as you wish and send it.

SAVING MESSAGES

A message will stay in the In box until you delete it. However, there may be times when you'd like to save it in a special mailbox, properly identified. To do this, either highlight the message on the In box summary display or open the message. You can then select New from the Transfer menu. The New Mailbox Dialog box is displayed as shown in Figure 2.8.

You can name the dialog box whatever you want. You can name it Yolanda, for instance, to save all messages from Yolanda. It will be created as a file with extension .mbx in the folder (or directory) on your hard drive where Eudora is located. That is, the Yolanda mailbox is the file yolanda.mbx. If you want the mailbox to be placed in a directory other than the one where Eudora is located, specify what you want to call the directory and then click on the box in front of Make it a Folder. You will create a directory by that name. You can then specify the name of the mailbox. Also, if all you want to do is to create the mailbox, but not transfer the currently selected mail into the mailbox, click on the box in front of "Don't transfer, just create a mailbox." You can then click on OK to complete the command.

NOTE: If you look at the directory structure, you will notice that all mailboxes are files with extension .mbx. For example, the In box is the file in.mbx and the Out box is out.mbx. If you want to delete a mailbox, just delete the corresponding file from the directory.

When you select the Mailbox menu next time, you will see Yolanda as one of the options in the drop-down menu. When you select a mailbox in the pulldown menu, the same summary as the one you saw for the In box is displayed. To view a message, double-click on it. The only exception is the Out box. When you open a message from an Out box, however, you will see a composition window so that you can continue working on the outgoing message.

FIGURE 2.8

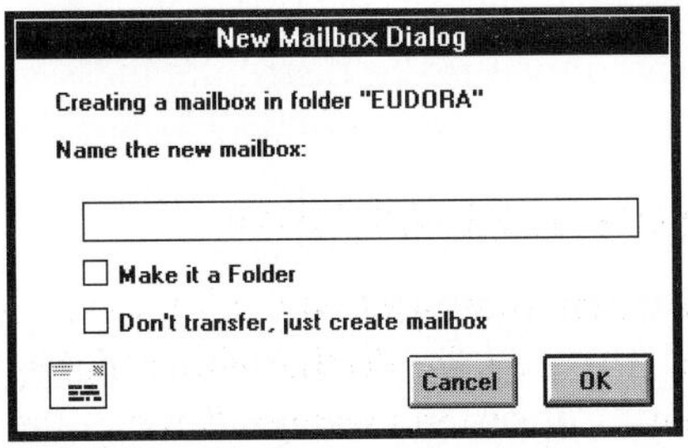

New Mailbox Dialog

Creating a mailbox in folder "EUDORA"

Name the new mailbox:

☐ Make it a Folder

☐ Don't transfer, just create mailbox

Cancel　OK

DELETING MESSAGES

As mentioned earlier, messages are stored indefinitely in any mailbox until you explicitly delete or transfer them to another mailbox. Outgoing messages that have been saved in the Out mailbox remain there until you send or delete them.

To delete a message, either highlight it in the summary listing or open it. You can then select <u>D</u>elete from the <u>M</u>essage menu or press (CTRL)-**D**.

If you have inadvertently deleted a message that you wish to keep, do not worry. This is a Windows application, after all. Deleted messages are placed in the Trash mailbox and are not deleted until you exit Eudora. You can select the <u>T</u>rash box option in the Mailbo<u>x</u> menu and transfer the message back into the desired mailbox.

NOTE:	If you notice that Trash is never emptied, select <u>S</u>witches from the <u>S</u>pecial menu. You can set the switch to empty trash when you exit Eudora.

   Exit Eudora.

EFFECTIVE E-MAIL

To some, e-mail appears to just be a faster way of delivering letters. Others think of e-mail as a substitute for telephone communication because of its rapidity: Messages can often be sent and replied to within minutes. However, e-mail is a mode of communication that is different from both postal and telephone systems, having its own advantages and drawbacks. Ironically, some of the advantages of e-mail are also drawbacks.

E-mail gets a message from one point to another very quickly, and, at least to the user, it is often much cheaper than using a telephone for instant long-distance communication. Furthermore, the sender can send it when it's convenient and the recipient can read it when he or she finds time. Hence, the time and distance differences are of little consequence. On the other hand, no matter how quickly a message may arrive at its destination, it makes no difference unless the receiver checks his or her e-mail on a regular basis.

E-mail makes it easy to forward or distribute messages, but because it is so easy, junk mail is sent to a large number of people. For instance, chain letters can flood the network and take up storage on the recipient's host computer. Remember, e-mail is not removed until the recipient deletes it, so think twice before forwarding messages to large numbers of people.

E-mail is ideal for informal discussions and quick responses. However, it is a *written* form of communication, so individuals are more accountable for what they write than with spoken communication. Many people tend to drift into informality in their messages and do not spend the time needed to construct a formal message. Furthermore, your messages might be saved by those who receive them, and they might later hold you accountable for rash words. They may even forward them on to others, to your potential embarrassment.

On the Internet, one person's e-mail message looks just like another, and often conveys little information about that person. Age, nationality, sex, or other factors which may influence face-to-face communication are not immediately apparent. Sometimes users forget that there really is a living person at the other end. Messages can become informal, impersonal, or curt, or, at the other extreme, too personal or involved. All the etiquette one may practice in face-to-face or even written communication may be forgotten or become secondary in electronic communication, and careless comments can lead to misunderstanding or ill feelings.

Also, security is low on e-mail communication. For example, a mail message that could not be delivered is returned to the sender. It's more likely, however, that the message is also returned to the administrator of the host computer where you have the account. You should never write an e-mail message that you wouldn't want to become public knowledge. Finally, you should be aware that it is possible—and not very difficult—to "forge" e-mail. So, if you get a message from someone that seems out of character, check with the sender before replying with an attack. He or she may not have sent the message, and you may be the victim of a malicious prank!

BOX 2.7

MAKING FACES

Because in e-mail it is difficult to add tone and context to e-mail messages, users on the Internet have adopted some conventions to use when making jokes or speaking lightheartedly. Some people will put remarks in <> brackets. For example, they might write "That was an awful party <hee hee>" or <grin> or just <g>. Also, some users draw pictures of smiling or winking faces, called "smilies" or "emoticons."

Here are some examples—note that you have to look at these pictures sideways—the colon or semicolon forms the eyes.

:)	happy
:(	sad
;)	wink
:P	sticking tongue out

Some faces can get rather complicated. Use your imagination!

After you use e-mail for a while, you'll see a lot of messages that should never have been sent, or ones the sender probably regrets. To prevent making such mistakes yourself, use the following guidelines.

✦ Never send an e-mail message that you wouldn't want to become public knowledge.

✦ Keep the length of each line reasonable (fewer than 60 characters) to make sure that each line is viewable from any terminal. Displayed line length is different depending on the terminal and the software being used, and sometimes this results in text being chopped off.

✦ Don't send abusive, harassing, or bigoted messages.

✦ Senders may approach e-mail as friendly, informal conversation, but recipients frequently view e-mail as a cast-in-stone message. You can't control how the receiver will perceive your message—so be careful.

✦ Use both upper- and lowercase characters. Messages written in all uppercase seem to be harsh, like shouting. All lowercase is too informal at times.

✦ Be careful with sarcasm or jokes. Readers cannot see your facial expressions or hear the tone of your voice.

✦ When responding to a message with multiple recipients, be very careful to whom you are responding. Usually, there is an option to either respond to the sender alone or to also respond to all the recipients listed. You do not want to be embarrassed by accidentally sending copies of your personal message to a group of people for whom the message was never intended. On the other hand, if you are continuing a group conversation, you'll want to be sure that you are replying to everyone.

✦ Read your message before you send it and decide if you'll regret it later. Most systems do not allow you to take back (cancel) what you've sent.

The intention here is not to dissuade you from using e-mail; rather, it is to make sure that you make effective, educated use of the mail. E-mail is a powerful and useful Internet tool.

WHAT'S A LISTSERV?

As mentioned earlier, you can contact friends and acquaintances using e-mail. This is an exciting and fun way to stay in touch, but there is more you can do with e-mail. You can join a discussion group, sometimes called an **e-conference**, utilizing **listservs**, also known as **list processors**, **mail reflectors**, or **mailing lists**.

The idea behind a listserv is that there is one address to which people can send mail, and that mail, in turn, is redistributed to everyone whose address appears *on the mailing list* (hence the name *listserv*, which stands for list server, or list processor). To be included on the list, a user **subscribes** to the list by sending a message to the listserv that manages that particular list. Once you subscribe to the list, you can send a message, or **post** a message, to the list. That message is then redistributed by the listserv to everyone that has subscribed to the list. A listserv may manage more than one list.

There are literally thousands of listservs. Topics discussed on a list can be anything about which a group of people might want to talk. For example, there are listservs on Albert Einstein's writings, superheroes in science fiction literature, various types of music, ecology and biospheres, World War II, and medicinal and aromatic plants, to name but a few. Some lists are designed for very practical discussions, others are more scholarly, and some are just plain silly. Of course, one's evaluation of what one finds interesting is personal.

A listserv is not just for discussion. It can also be used as a resource for getting answers to your questions. You can post a message asking for a particular piece of information, and within a few hours, other subscribers will reply with answers. Also, some lists are used to distribute **electronic journals (e-journals)** and **electronic newsletters (e-newsletters)**. An e-journal is much like a print journal, only instead of coming to your postal address in print format, it arrives at your e-mail address in electronic format. You can probably guess what e-newsletters are. You can subscribe to receive an e-journal or e-newsletter in the same way that you subscribe to a discussion group.

Listservs are a powerful communication tool, as they can put you in contact with others who have similar interests, even if they are thousands of miles away. As a student, you may want to find listservs pertaining to the subjects you are studying. This will give you an opportunity to exchange views with and help other students in finding resources.

HOW DO I SUBSCRIBE TO A LISTSERV?

As with most Internet resources, there are several different types of listservs. The following instructions should work for the majority of lists out there, but we will also tell you of a few variations that you might run into.

To subscribe to a list, you need to know a couple of things: (1) the name of the list; (2) the address of the listserv that manages the list; and (3) instructions on how to subscribe. It may not hurt to know (4) how to **unsubscribe** from the list.

Suppose you wanted to sign up for a discussion group called esgti-l (which stands for every student's guide to the internet—list) managed by the listserv at willamette.edu. This is an actual discussion group for people using this book!

NOTE:	Many, but not all, list names end in a -l for *list*. (This is the lowercase letter L, and not the number one.)

Here's the tricky part about listservs. You have to distinguish between when you should send a message to the *listserv* (which is the program managing things like subscription requests) and the *list* (which will distribute the message to the subscribers). The address of the listserv is listproc@willamette.edu, while the address of the list is esgti-l@willamette.edu. The listserv address is where you can send commands to subscribe and unsubscribe. The list address is where you send messages that you wish everyone on the list to receive.

Many of the listserv addresses are on **BITNET**,[1] as listservs originated on the BITNET. BITNET addresses do not end in standard Internet geographical or administrative domain names, such as edu, gov, com, and net. In most cases, all you need to do to send mail to a BITNET address from the Internet is to add **.bitnet** at the end of the BITNET address. For example, if the address is listserv@tamvm1, then address it to listserv@tamvm1.bitnet. If your host computer does not understand the use of .bitnet (if your message bounced or was lost), you must use the format "listserv%host.bitnet@<*an.interbit.gateway*>," where <*an.interbit.gateway*> is one of the following:

cornellc.cit.cornell.edu
cunyvm.cuny.edu
mitvma.mit.edu
vm1.nodak.edu

The address in the previous example becomes listserv%tamvm1.bitnet@cunyvm.cuny.edu. The same applies to the mailing addresses of the lists themselves.

NOTE:	On the Internet, the program listproc (list processor) is used (instead of listserv) more often. On a list processor, subscription messages should be sent to *listproc* rather than to listserv. However, many of the systems supporting list processors are set up so that if you send mail to listserv, the system will forward the message to listproc.

To subscribe to a list, send a mail message to the listserv address with the message:

subscribe <*listname*> <*your name*>

---

[1] BITNET ("Because It's Time Net") is a network founded in 1981 to link universities and other academic institutions that didn't at that time have ARPA or NFSNET access. By 1988 there were over 1,500 nodes in the network, up from 65 in 1983. BITNET uses a different network and transmission protocol and relies heavily on e-mail to move information back and forth (whereas TCP/IP networks can support non-mail applications such as FTP and Gopher). The listserv software was originally written for BITNET sites and still supports a large user base.

where *<listname>* is the name of the list and *<your name>* is really your name. That is, if your name is Cheryl Brown, type **Cheryl Brown**. There is no need to enter the subject line.

 Subscribe to the list esgti-l at Willamette University. Willamette University uses listproc rather than listserv. For example, if your name is Cheryl Brown, you would send the following e-mail:

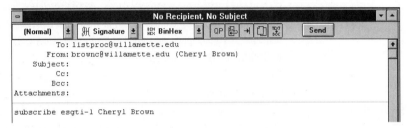

You will receive a message back from the listserv confirming that you are subscribed and giving you additional information about the list. This includes information about how to unsubscribe to the list. Keep this information around. From this point on, you will receive any mail that anyone sends to esgti-l @willamette.edu!

 Send a message to the list. Remember, send this message to the list address, esgti-l @willamette.edu. Everyone subscribed to the list will receive a copy of your message.

NOTE: Sometimes a list will not send a copy of the message to the person who posted it. A list will only send you a copy of messages that you post if your mail is set to "ACK"nowledge. See Table 2.1 for commands to set listproc and listserv features.

A word of caution: Some lists are very busy, with many messages being posted in a short time. It is easy for your mailbox to become very full very fast! If you do not or cannot check your mail on a regular basis, you should not subscribe to a list. If you are going on a vacation, consider either unsubscribing or temporarily stopping mail from the list. If your mailbox becomes embarrassingly overstuffed, your local system administrator may just do something about it!

To unsubscribe from a list, send an e-mail message to the listserv address with the following message:

unsubscribe *<listname>*

where *<listname>* is the name of the list from which you wish to unsubscribe.

 Unsubscribe from esgti-l at Willamette University. Remember, send the message to the listserv, not to esgti-l.

Table 2.1 lists other commands you can send to the listserv.

As mentioned earlier, once you have subscribed to a list, you can begin posting messages to it. Note that some lists allow anyone to post, others will accept postings only from subscribers, and still others are **moderated**, meaning that there is a moderator who reads all incoming postings to make sure they are appropriate for the list. He or she decides which messages actually get distributed.

NOTE: If you'd like to subscribe to the list esgti-l at Willamette University, do so. As mentioned earlier, this is a real discussion group for people using this book. You can ask questions of the authors or discuss topics with other readers.

BUT WAIT

Because messages sent to a mailing list can get distributed to literally thousands of people, it is wise to think about the types of messages you post. Hence all of the rules of etiquette described earlier apply here, only more so. There are two commonly made mistakes in using a listserv. One is to send a message to the list

---

TABLE 2.1 LISTSERV COMMANDS

Here is a brief list of some of the other commands that most listservs will accept. Remember, these commands must be sent to the listserv@ address!

subscribe *<listname> <your name>*	Subscribes you to the list
unsubscribe *<listname>*	Unsubscribes you to the list
review *<listname>*	Sends you a list of all the people who are subscribed to the list
index *<listname>*	Sends back the names of any files that are archived on the list
info *<listname>*	Often this command will result in an informational file about the listserv being sent to you, which can be useful in determining what commands and mail options are valid
get *<filename>*	Gets a file that is archived on the listserv and sends it to you via e-mail
set *<listname>* nomail	Temporarily stops mail from the list
set *<listname>* mail	Restarts mail after temporarily stopping mail
set *<listname>* repro	Has the listserv send you a copy of whatever you post to the list

The final three commands above don't work on all lists. If you try and the listserv rejects your command, try using:

set *<listname>* mail postpone	Stops mail
set *<listname>* mail ack	Restores mail. The "ack" (for "acknowledge") is the equivalent of "repro" in the above list.

when you meant the listserv, or vice-a-versa; and the other is to reply to the entire list rather than to just the sender.

Remember, you send a message to the listserv when you want to subscribe, unsubscribe, or give other commands (as listed in Table 2.1). Send mail to the list when you want to post a message to the entire list. If you accidentally send mail meant for the list to the listserv instead, it will be ignored as the listserv will not recognize it. However, if you accidentally send mail meant for the listserv to the list, the entire list membership will see your "unsubscribe" (or whatever command you sent) message, which can be embarrassing!

When a message is distributed by the listserv, an extra line appears on the header: Reply to: <*listname*>. When you reply to e-mail, you have a choice of sending a reply to the list or to the sender (poster). Make sure that you know to whom you are responding. You do not want to send a personal message to the entire list.

One thing you may want to do when you first subscribe to a list is to observe and find out the tone and flavor of the list. Each list has different personality and, often, its own set of etiquette and protocol. It's good to find out these things before posting. The name or the description of the list can be quite misleading. If the list did not turn out to be what you had in mind, simply unsubscribe.

As with any group of people, there are sometimes inappropriate, if not downright nasty, exchanges on mailing lists. These are sometimes referred to as **flame wars**. If you notice these, the best action is not to get involved. If you feel you want to say something, send a personal message to the individual. Being involved in a flame war can be a fantastic waste of time, and does no good for your cyber reputation! You never know where your e-mail may end up, and imagine your surprise when, years from now, you are on a job interview and your potential employer says, "Hey, aren't you the person who ranted and raved on. . . ." As mentioned before, think twice before posting a message. Sometimes folks on a list will surround their extreme comments with "flame on" and "flame off," just to let others know that they are aware of what they are doing.

All warnings aside, posting to lists can be a great way to exchange ideas, ask and answer questions, and get to know others on the Internet who share your interests. When dealt with wisely, they can be an astoundingly rich resource.

Many listservs offer one more feature: The ability to electronically search and retrieve files that are archived under listserv. You will be doing this in the next section.

WHERE'S THE LIST?

You may be asking yourself, "How can I find out what lists and e-journals are available?" If you want a fairly comprehensive list of all lists, you can obtain the

global list from (where else?) a listserv, using its electronic search and retrieval capability. To get a complete list, you can send the message:

list global

to listserv@kentvm.kent.edu. The subject line must be left blank.

| **BOX 2.8** | **THE DIRECTORY OF SCHOLARLY CONFERENCES** |

Another source of lists is "The Directory of Scholarly Conferences" edited by Diane Kovacs. This directory contains descriptions of e-conferences on topics of interest to scholars. *E-conference* is an umbrella term that includes discussion lists, Internet interest groups, e-journals, e-newsletters, and so on.

The directory is available online via Gopher (discussed in Chapter 4) and anonymous FTP (covered in Chapter 6). After you study those chapters, you can follow the directions given at the bottom and locate some interesting e-conferences. The directory is composed of the following files:

Filename	Filetype	Description of Content and Size
ACADLIST	FILE1	(Anthropology—Education) 85k
ACADLIST	FILE2	(Geography—Library and Information Science) 115k
ACADLIST	FILE3	(Linguistics—Political Science) 64k
ACADLIST	FILE4	(Psychology—Writing) 68k
ACADLIST	FILE5	(Biological Sciences) 55k
ACADLIST	FILE6	(Physical Sciences) 51k
ACADLIST	FILE7	(Business, Academia, News) 31k
ACADLIST	FILE8	(Computer Science; Social, Cultural, and Political Aspects of Computing; and Academic Computing Support) 139k
ACADWHOL	HQX	(Binhexed self-decompressing Macintosh MS Word 5.0 document of whole directory) 799k

When you receive a file, you will find a list of e-conferences covering subject areas indicated above. Each entry (for a listserv) on the list includes:

LN: e-conference name and submission address
TI: topic information
SU: subscription information
ED: edited? Yes or no (private lists were called *edited*)
AR: archived? If yes, frequency; Private means by subscription only
MO: moderator, editor, listowner, manager, coordinator
IA: "official" institutional affiliation
KE: keywords

Continued on next page

BOX 2.8

THE DIRECTORY OF SCHOLARLY CONFERENCES (*continued*)

A typical entry reads as follows:

LN: CERRO-L@AEARN
TI: Central European REgional Research Organization. CERRO-L
is an e-conference discussing issues of relevance to regional
development and regional development research in Central
Europe. CERRO-L discusses topics from a broad range of
related disciplines: regional science, economic geography,
regional and urban planning, environmental economics,
regional sociology, policy analysis, regional political
economy and institutions, etc. It is the intention of CERRO-L
to stimulate and support regional research in and about the
newly re-emerging regions of "Central Europe" and to enhance
contacts and discussion between researchers and scholars
interested in these areas.
SU: (EARN) LISTSERV@AEARN (Internet)
LISTSERV@AEARN.EDVZ.UNILINZ.AC.AT
ED: No
AR: Yes, available via anonymous ftp to ftp.wu-wien.ac.at cd pub/cerro
MO: Gerhard Gonter (Bitnet) GONTER@AWIWUW11—Gunther Maier
(Bitnet) CERRO@AWIWUW11 (Internet) GUNTHER.MAIER@WU-
WIEN.AC.AT
IA: University of Economics and Business Administration,
Vienna, Austria Slovak Academy of Sciences, Bratislava, CSFR
University of North Carolina at Chapel Hill, Chapel Hill, NC,
USA
KE: Central European Research

RETRIEVE FILES VIA GOPHER

You can use the keyword "ACADLIST" to do a Veronica search of directory titles, or you can go through gopher.willamette.edu. From the Willamette University menu, select "Library Resources," "Electronic Books and Journals," "Electronic Journals," and then "Directory of Scholarly Electronic Conferences."

RETRIEVE FILES VIA ANONYMOUS FTP

Use anonymous FTP to get to ksuvxa.kent.edu. First enter **cd library** then **get *filename.filetype***, where *filename*=acadlist and *filetype*=file1 (file2, and so on).

The file you receive in return is quite large—360,000 words or more, which totals more than 100 printed pages. You will probably prefer to search the global list for discussion groups on a particular subject by adding the option /<*topic*> where <*topic*> is one or more words describing the subject in which you are interested. Let's say that you are interested in finding listservs that deal with languages.

 Send an e-mail to listserv@kentvm.kent.edu. Leave the subject line blank, with the body of the message as follows:

list global /language

At the time of writing this book, a list of 51 listservs was returned. This number may well have increased.

Each line in the global list contains a list's name, the BITNET address of the list, and a brief description of the topics discussed in that list. For example, the reply from the above online exercise included:

Listname	Address	Description
APLIEM-L	APLIEM-L@BRUFU	Association of English Language Teachers
FLAC-L	FLAC-L@BROWNVM	Foreign Language Across Curriculum List
GAELIC-L	GAELIC-L@IRLEARN	Gaelic Language Bulletin Board
NIHONGO	NIHONGO@MITVMA	Japanese Language Discussion List
SLLING-L	SLLING-L@YALEVM	Sign Language Linguistics List
WHIRL	WHIRL@PSUVM	Women's History in Rhetoric and Language

BOX 2.9   LISTSERV SAMPLINGS

Literally thousands of listservs are available. It would be impossible to list those of interest to everyone. Also, the titles are not always representative of the content, and there is no guarantee that a list is active. The following is a sampling of mailing lists in various disciplines.

Description	Listname and Address
Academic Advising—Higher Education	ACADV@NDSUVM1
African Cultures	AFRICA-L@BRUFMG
African American Students	AASNET-L@UHUPVM1
Albert Einstein	EPP-L@BUACCA
Anthropology Research Techniques	ANTHRO-L@UBVM

Continued on next page

BOX 2.9

LISTSERV SAMPLINGS (*continued*)

Description	Listname and Address
Archaeology—Archaeology Software News	ARCH-L@DGOGWDG1
Art History—Architectural History	CAAH@PUCC
Chemistry research	CHEMIC-L@TAUNIVM
China—Chinese Culture	CHINA@PUCC
Cinema Film Criticism	CINEMA-L@AUVM
Economics Business	ECONED-L@UTDALLAS
Fluid Mechanics	BURG-CEN@HEARN
Folklore—Cross-Cultural Studies	FOLKLORE@TAMVM1
Hebrew Langauge—Jewish Culture —Near East Studies	HEBREW-L@UMINN1
History	HISTORY@UWAVM
Holmes, Sherlock Literature	HOUND@BELOIT.EDU
Humanities and Computers	CHUG-L@BROWNVM
Ireland—Irish Research	IRL-NET@IRLEARN
Japan—Japanese Culture	JPINFO-L@JPNSUT00
Latin American Studies	MCLR-L@MSU
Linear Algebra	ILAS-NET@TECHNION
Music, Classical—Music Research	CLASSM-L@BROWNVM
Philosophy	FNORD-L@UBVM
Photography	PHOTO-L@BUACCA
Photosynthesis	PHOTOSYN@NET.BIO.NET
Physics	PHYSICS@MIAMIU
Play—Games—Sport	PLAY-L@HG.ULETH.CA
Polish News—Poland	POLAND@NDCVX.CC.ND.EDU
Politics	POLITICS@UCF1VM
Postmodern Culture—Postmodern Literature	PMC-LIST@NCSUVM
Psychology—Human Development	CCHD-L@UNCVM1
Religious Studies	RELIGION@HARVARDA
Renaissance Studies—Reformation Studies	FICINO@UTORONTO
Russia—Russian Culture	RUSSIA@ARIZVM1
Slovak Culture	SLOVAK-L@UBVM
Southern United States Cultural Studies—Humor	BUBBA-L@KNUTH.MTSU.EDU
Student Government Universities	SGANET@VTVM1
Superheroes Science Fiction Literature	SUPERGUY@UCF1VM

BOX 2.10

WHAT DID THEY SAY BEFORE ME?

Although much useful information can be discussed on a listserv, unless you happened to be reading the list when a topic was brought up, you may miss it entirely! Sometimes you will be referred to a previous discussion on the list when you ask a question. You may be wondering how to get a copy of past postings to the list. Many, but by no means all, BITNET listservs and UNIX listprocs maintain archives of all list correspondence which can be searched using e-mail.

BITNET LISTSERV

If you know that you are dealing with a BITNET-style listserv (the information sheet about the list should enlighten you on this subject, or give you the address of someone who can), you can use the following commands. Send a message to the *listserv* address (not to the *list* address):

```
//
database search dd=rules
//rules dd *
search <keyword(s)> in <list>
index
/*
```

In this command, *<keyword(s)>* are the words that you seek, and *<list>* is the name of the list to search. For example, to send the keyword "conference" in a list called nettrain, enter:

```
//database search dd=rules
//rules dd*
search conference in nettrain
index
/*
```

After sending this message, you should receive a message from the listserv containing an access number and the subject line of all messages that contained your keyword or words. To retrieve the messages you wish to read, send the following command in an e-mail message to the listserv, with the same keywords and list name, and the numbers (*number1, number2, . . .*) or the message that you wish to retrieve.

```
//
database search dd=rules
//rules dd *
```

Continued on next page

BOX 2.10

WHAT DID THEY SAY BEFORE ME? (*continued*)

search <*keyword(s)*> in <*list*>
print all of <*number1*> <*number2*> ...
/*

For example, to receive messages 003283 and 003236 from the previous example, type:

//database search dd=rules
//rules dd *
search conference in nettrain
print all of 003283 003236
/*

If this does not work for the list you wish to search, send the command **info** to the listserv for any searching information local to that listserv.

UNIX LISTPROC

To search a listproc list, send the following command to the listproc address:

search <*list*> "<*keyword*>"

<*list*> is the name of the list, and <*keyword*> is the word for which you are searching. You should get a reply from the listproc listing all the files in that list's archive, with each line in that file in which the keyword appears. Listprocs do not always store messages individually; sometimes a week's or month's worth of messages is lumped together in one file. You can read through looking for lines of text that seem to relate to your subject. When you have a file or two picked out that you would like to retrieve, send the following command to the listproc:

get <*list*> <*filename*>

Enter the filename exactly as it appears in the text, because generally the listproc is not quite "smart" enough to figure out which file you mean. The file will be returned to you by the listproc; be ready for a potentially huge file. If the list in question is high-volume, you may receive quite a bit of text in your mailbox.

If these commands don't get any results, send the command **info** to the listproc for information about that listproc.

Should you decide to subscribe to the Japanese Language Discussion List, send the subscription message as described earlier to listserv@mitvma.bitnet. Once subscribed, you can post your messages to nihongo@mitvma.bitnet.

Another approach which can yield useful results is to search the archives of the listserv new-list@vm1.nodak.edu (see Box 2.10 on searching listserv archives). new-list announces the creation of new lists, appropriately enough. To keep abreast of new lists as they become available, you may want to subscribe to this list.

Several commercial publications also list mailing lists. You can check for these in your local library. You should be aware that none of these lists is comprehensive. There may always be mailing lists that are listed in one place, but not in another, and some that are not listed at all! However, these techniques should help you find the types of lists for which you are searching.

SUMMARY

In this chapter, many of the terms and concepts that are necessary to use e-mail and listservs are introduced:

✦ E-mail is a system for sending messages or files to the accounts of other computer users.

✦ In order to use the e-mail capability on the Internet, you must know the recipient's e-mail address and how to use the e-mail program.

✦ An e-mail address is composed of the username and the domain name separated by an at (@) sign.

✦ The Internet does not yet offer an easy, standardized way to find everyone's e-mail address.

✦ Advantages offered by e-mail can also be its drawbacks. Hence, one must learn effective use of e-mail.

✦ Listserv is an electronic discussion forum based on mail distribution that can also be used to distribute e-journals and e-newsletters.

✦ To subscribe to a list on a listserv, you need to find the name of the list and the address of the listserv that manages that particular list. You can then send the subscription message to the listserv.

✦ Messages for distribution on a list must be mailed to the list address, not to the listserv address.

✦ To receive a complete list of lists (on listservs), you can send the message **list global** to listserv@kentvm.kent.edu. To limit the search to a specific topic, add the option **/<topic>**, where *<topic>* is one or more words describing the subject in which you are interested.

KEY TERMS

address	flame war	Netfind
ASCII file	global list	plain text file
BITNET	hostname	POP mail
CSO server	list processor	POP mail server
domain name	listserv	post
e-conference	mail reflector	subscribe
e-journal	mailing list	unsubscribe
e-newsletter	moderated list	username

REVIEW QUESTIONS

1. What is the standard format for an e-mail address on the Internet?

2. Is there an easy way to find someone's e-mail address?

3. What do you need to know in order to send an e-mail message?

4. What are the advantages of using e-mail?

5. What are the drawbacks of using e-mail?

6. What is a listserv?

7. You decided to subscribe to a list called new-list, located at vm1.nodak.edu. How do you subscribe to that list?

8. When do you send a message to the listserv? to the list itself?

9. What is the difference between a discussion list and an e-journal?

10. What message do you send to receive a file listing all lists (on listservs) pertaining to psychology?

EXERCISES

1. Send an e-mail message to your instructor with a carbon copy to one classmate.

2. Locate the name and address of a mailing list about Eastern Europe.

3. You can receive White House press releases in the form of an e-newsletter. Send mail to clinton-info@campaign92.org with the subject line **Help**. What sort of information did you receive? What would you need to do to begin receiving White House press releases about the economy via e-mail?

4. Let's say that there was a discussion earlier on a listserv you subscribe to about some of the more famous names on the 'net. You didn't save the messages, but now you've run across one of them, this Kibo person, in a couple of other places, and you'd like to retrieve that information again. How would you go about getting those messages from the listserv?

5. You've come across the listserv called envst-l, a list discussing environmental studies programs, but the address that you've found includes only envst-l@brownvm and listserv@brownvm. What does this mean? Specify how to subscribe to this listserv.

DISCUSSION TOPICS

1. Discuss the advantages and drawbacks of e-mail. Give examples of messages that may be misperceived.

2. Discuss benefits a student would gain by subscribing to a mailing list.

3. Why might people interpret things differently when they come in the form of: e-mail, "real" mail, or face-to-face conversation?

4. You've received an e-mail chain letter in your mailbox. Some other user has sent copies of a letter to numerous acquaintances or even just random addresses. What is the best thing to do, and why?

USENET NEWSGROUPS
Bulletin Board Services of the Internet

CHAPTER 3

OBJECTIVES

Upon completing the material presented in this chapter, you should understand the following aspects of the Internet:

✦ The concept behind Usenet
✦ How to use a news reader program
✦ How to start a news reader program
✦ How to find a newsgroup
✦ How to subscribe and unsubscribe to a newsgroup
✦ How to read news articles
✦ How to respond to news articles

BEFORE YOU START

In order to perform online exercises in this chapter, you need the following:

✦ An account on a computer with access to the Internet
✦ An IBM PC compatible running Windows and connected to the Internet
✦ A copy of the WinVN program installed on the Windows computer you are using. The one used here is WinVN Version 0.93.11.

WHAT'S USENET?

Suppose for a moment that each morning when you wake and grab a glass of orange juice, you are presented with a wide selection of newspapers from which to read. These papers range in quality from serious national and international newspapers to local school papers to supermarket tabloids. You browse these papers scanning for your favorite topics, reading bits here and there, and maybe even cutting out the articles which you find interesting. Now imagine that not only can you *read* these newspapers, you can also *reply* in them. You can even start a new topic of discussion. This is what **Usenet** is all about: It is a collection of thousands of topically organized **newsgroups** in which you can both discover and expound (or even blather) on topical information.

Although Usenet is often referred to as newsgroups, **netnews**, or just plain **news**, it isn't the same as a newspaper; at a newspaper, an editor generally controls what people write. Although your site can, for a fee, pick up a **news feed** from a commercial service such as Clarinet (which distributes United Press International and other wire services electronically over Usenet), the vast majority of newsgroups are written by users on the Internet discussing topics that interest them. This doesn't stop people from referring to the information which gets distributed via Usenet as **articles**, however. Sometimes there is a **moderator**, someone who reviews the articles before they are distributed and keeps folks in line, but most groups function as an open forum on a topic, much as you would hear if the participants were all talking together in the same room over cups of cappuccino. The topics of discussion can range from nuclear physics to artificial intelligence to vegetarian recipes for chili to the latest soap opera. It is a good place for browsing and doesn't require a lot of commitment.

After reading the chapter on listservs, you may be asking yourself, "Isn't this what listservs are for?" Well, yes, listservs serve much the same purpose, and you can even read some listserv lists via Usenet. The big difference is that with a listserv, all **postings**, or submissions, are sent directly to your mailbox (and if you don't delete your mail, they accumulate); with newsgroups, you can wander into the newsgroup discussion when you have time. Just as with listservs and mailing lists, you can subscribe and unsubscribe to newsgroups. However, unlike with mailing lists, if you don't read the articles, they'll just disappear after a few days.

Because this isn't e-mail, you will have to learn how to use additional software. As with most Internet tools, there are several news reader software packages from which you can choose. For Windows systems, a popular news reader is WinVN, which is a very easy to use, yet robust, news reader program. A news reader program helps you keep track of the news items you have already seen and displays new items that have arrived since your last session. The program even lists newly formed newsgroups and asks if you are interested in reading them. WinVN also

threads the articles in each newsgroup. Threads allow you to read news items in order within a topic, based on what appears as the subject line of the article. While newsgroups organize articles loosely by subject, threads further organize topics by collecting all articles in that group with the same subject line.

WHO MANAGES NEWSGROUPS?

Anyone on the Internet can start a newsgroup on any topic of interest. Although there are some moderated newsgroups, in general, newsgroups are a forum where almost anything goes. In fact, articles in a newsgroup may not even stay on the supposed subject of the group. It is up to the users to use forums wisely! No one person or organization controls or regulates newsgroups. For the most part, it is an open and uncensored environment.

News is received through news feeds. At each site, a person, known as the **news administrator**, or a group is responsible for what newsgroups a site receives and how the news feed is operated. A site may choose to restrict the flow of news or to receive every conceivable newsgroup. A typical site subscribes to over 1,500 newsgroups.

The news administrator also decides how long to keep news articles. This depends on factors such as the amount of local space available to store the newsgroup articles and the amount of traffic on the particular newsgroup. A news article may be stored for just a few days or up to months. If you don't look at a newsgroup for awhile, you will miss topics of discussion as they come and go.

NEWSGROUP ORGANIZATION

There are literally thousands of newsgroups, and new ones appear daily. Also, as you might have realized by now, they do not necessarily contain "news" as we usually think of it. Newsgroup articles are not the same kind of articles that you might find in your newspaper. Rather, these are discussion groups, classified ads, announcements, and just plain old bulletin board services. Fortunately, the topics are broken down by groups, so you can select the ones of greatest interest to you. Group names are often three or more words long, separated by dots. The first word provides a very general description of the group, and each following word becomes more and more specific. Unlike listservs, the name does not reflect the origin of the newsgroup. For example, the newsgroup sci.bio.ecology stands for a *science* group, focusing on *bio*logy, with an emphasis on *ecology*. You could reasonably expect to find discussions of the effects of acid rain on lake fish or the decline of songbirds in North America in this newsgroup. Table 3.1 lists some types of newsgroups.

TABLE 3.1   SOME TYPES OF NEWSGROUPS

alt	*alt*ernative, and sometimes silly or extreme discussion
bit	*bit*net listservs—many listservs are available via Usenet. The names follow a bit-*listserv.listname* scheme.
clari	*clari*net news service—a newswire service for which you must pay. You may or may not have access from your site.
comp	*comp*uter topics, including use, purchase, and programming
de	*de*utsch—technical, recreational, and social discussion in German
gnu	Discussions related to the Free Software Foundation (FSF) and its *GNU* project
K12	For students in *K*indergarten through *12*th grade, or discussions about that group on the 'net
misc	*misc*ellaneous—meaning exactly that! This contains newsgroups that don't fit under other headings.
news	*news*groups! Yes, these are newsgroups *about* newsgroups! Despite how ridiculous this may sound, groups such as news.newusers.questions might actually be good places to start.
rec	*rec*reational groups, including pastimes and sports groups
sci	*sci*ence topics—these can range from the very simple to the very serious
soc	*soc*iety, including foreign countries and cultures. Many of these lists are in foreign languages.

You will run into many other "top level" designations. For instance, some schools have newsgroups for different topics on campus, and will have their own local hierarchy. Willamette University has a set of newsgroups that starts with willamette, such as willamette.news or willamette.forsale, where the campus community can share information of local interest.

NOTE: When referring to a newsgroup name, a period is read as "dot." For example, willamette.news is read "willamette dot news."

USING A NEWS READER PROGRAM

To read newsgroups, you must have a news reader program installed on the computer you are using. Fortunately, news readers exist for nearly all major computer platforms. One of the more popular news readers for the Windows platform is WinVN, and we will use it for our examples. Regardless of the news reader you are using, the concepts presented here will still hold true.

In order to read newsgroups, you need to know the following: (1) how to start the news reader program; (2) how to select and subscribe to a newsgroup; (3) how to select an article to view; (4) how to respond to an article; and (5) how to quit the news reader. It may help to know (6) how to unsubscribe to a newsgroup as well.

STARTING AND QUITTING WINVN

 Visually locate the WinVN program icon in the Program Manager window. It should look similar to the one shown below.

Winvn

Start the WinVN program by double-clicking on the WinVN icon.

If you get the message "Not connected to news server," open the Network menu and select Connect to Server.

The WinVN program starts. Depending on how WinVN is configured, you may see the Request LIST from server? dialog box as shown in Figure 3.1.

NOTE: If you want to connect to the server automatically when WinVN is started, open the Config menu, select Communication, click on the selection box in front of Connect at startup, and click OK.

The dialog box asks whether you want to request the latest newsgroup list from the server. This list would include new newsgroups that have been created since the last time you used WinVN. If this is the first time this copy of WinVN is being run (since the installation), you will need to answer Yes. Otherwise, click on the No button.

 Click No or Yes accordingly. If the New Newsgroup dialog box appears, click on Cancel.

*The **Main Group-List window** similar to the one shown in Figure 3.2 is displayed.*

Quit the WinVN program as you would most Windows applications.

FIGURE 3.1

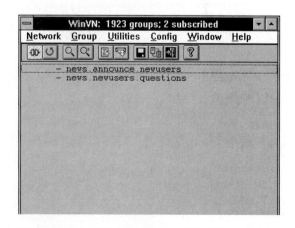

FIGURE 3.2

From the <u>N</u>etwork menu, select E<u>x</u>it or press (ALT)-(F4) (hold down the (ALT) key and press the (F4) function key).

The WinVN application is closed.

FINDING NEWSGROUPS

How can you find out what newsgroups are available? You can get a complete list of all newsgroups available to you by displaying the list of unsubscribed groups. The list follows the list of groups you are subscribed to and is usually quite long (remember that an average site subscribes to over 1,500 newsgroups).

Start WinVN. If necessary, open <u>N</u>etwork and select <u>C</u>onnect to Server.

If you see the Request LIST from server dialog box, click **No.**

The Main Group-List window is displayed again.

The list may display only the groups you are subscribed to, or it may also display all of the unsubscribed groups as well. The menu bar indicates the number of subscribed groups and unsubscribed groups.

FIGURE 3.3

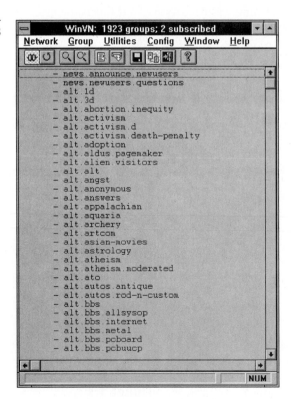

BOX 3.1

PERSONALIZING WINVN

In installing the WinVn program you are using, someone had to specify the News Server and the Mail Server—computers through which newsgroups and mail are received. The person also had to specify his or her identity—name, organization, and the e-mail address. The e-mail address is the one that is automatically inserted as the sender when you respond to a posting on the newsgroup.

If the computer you are using is yours and all information pertinent to you has been entered, there is no problem. However, if you are using someone else's computer, set up for his or her use, or if you are letting someone else use your computer to read and respond to the newsgroups, incorrect information can get distributed all over the Internet. Also, should you change the account to another Internet host computer or if your institution changes the News Server, you need to specify the change.

Do not despair. You can change all of this information through the Config menu. When you select this menu, you will see several commands for configuring WinVn. The Personal Info dialog box allows you to enter your name, e-mail address, and the name of your organization. Use the Communications dialog box to enter the names of your News Server and your Mail Server.

Now, if you changed this information on someone else's computer so that you could use it, be sure to change it back!

 If you don't see a long list, click on the Toggle display of unsubscribed groups button (▣) on the toolbar.

A screen similar to the one in Figure 3.3 is displayed. Note that there may be nearly 2,000 newsgroups!

You can take your time and browse through the list to see if any entries interest you, or you can use the Find command to look for specific kinds of newsgroups. Once you find a newsgroup of interest to you, you can either read it or subscribe to it.

Let's use the following scenario: You are interested in participating in discussions on the AIDS epidemic.

You could take a look and see if you can find anything under the science category. Remember, these groups have *sci* as the first word in their names, so all you need to do is to scroll the screen until you are in the *sci*ence category.

 Using the vertical scroll bar, scroll the screen so that newsgroups starting with *sci* are displayed.

The screen may be similar to the one shown in Figure 3.4.

FIGURE 3.4

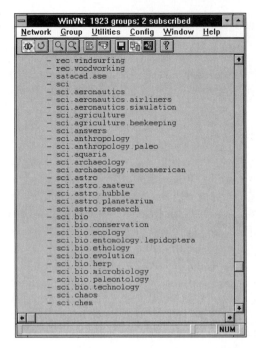

You can see that there are quite a few newsgroups that start with *sci*. So, let's try a more specific search using "aids" as the keyword.

From the Group menu, select Find or, press (CTRL)-F (hold down the (CTRL) key and press F). You can also click on the Search button (🔍) from the toolbar.

The Search for String dialog box is displayed, as shown in Figure 3.5.

Type **aids** then click on the OK button or press (ENTER).

A newsgroup whose name contains the word "aids" is highlighted, as shown in Figure 3.6. The list of newsgroups you see may not be identical to the one shown.

You can repeat the search by opening the Group menu and selecting Find Next or by pressing (F3). You can also click on the Find Next button on the toolbar. The keyword may appear in many newsgroup names.

READING A NEWSGROUP

To open a newsgroup, double-click on the newsgroup name. If there is a large number of articles posted to the newsgroup, WinVN will prompt you to enter the number of articles you'd like to see listed.

FIGURE 3.5

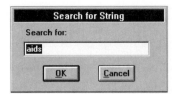

FIGURE 3.6

Find next ——

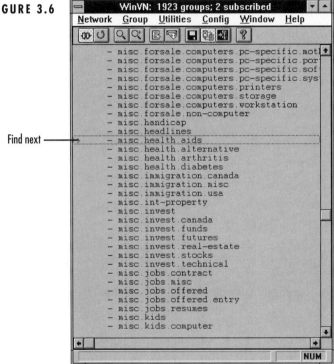

  Double-click on a newsgroup.

A screen similar to Figure 3.7 is displayed, listing articles posted to the newsgroup.

To open an article, double-click on the name of the article. The article is displayed in its own window. You can close the article by opening the File menu and selecting Exit or by double-clicking on the control-menu box on the top left corner of the window.

Once you start reading articles in a newsgroup, you can read the next article by opening the View menu and selecting Next Article or by pressing (CTRL)-**N**. You can also click on the View next article button ((▶)).

FIGURE 3.7

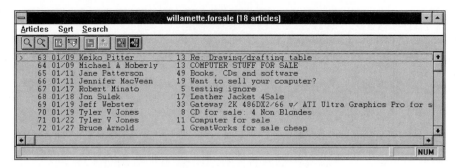

You can jump to the next thread (subject) by opening the <u>V</u>iew menu and selecting Next with same <u>S</u>ubject or by pressing [F3]. You can also click on the View next article with same subject button ([⌐]).

 Close the article window by opening <u>F</u>ile menu and selecting E<u>x</u>it or by double-clicking on the control-menu box. You can also click on the Close window button ([⊠]).

SUBSCRIBING TO NEWSGROUPS

When you **subscribe** to a newsgroup, the name is added to the list of subscribed groups, thus making it easier for you to find and open the newsgroup. Remember, you can toggle the display of unsubscribed groups by clicking on the Toggle button.

 Make sure the list of unsubscribed groups is displayed.

Select a newsgroup to which you wish to subscribe by clicking on the name.

From the <u>G</u>roup menu, select <u>S</u>ubscribe Selected Groups.

The newsgroup moves to the bottom of the subscribed group list.

Subscribe to as many groups as you wish by repeating the process.

NOTE: You can also make multiple selections by holding down the [CTRL] key as you click on several newsgroup names. You can then give the command to subscribe.

After you have finished subscribing to newsgroups, you can click on the display of unsubscribed groups button so that the unsubscribed groups list is not displayed.

READING SUBSCRIBED NEWSGROUPS

You can read *subscribed* newsgroups as you read newsgroups. However, there is an important difference: When you read subscribed groups, WinVN keeps track of which articles you have read, and will display only unread articles since you last opened that newsgroup.

When new users join the group, they often ask a question that has been asked and answered several times in the past. This can become tiresome for longtime followers of the group. To help out the new readers and to prevent the same topics from being discussed ad nauseum, most newsgroups have a list of Frequently Asked Questions. **FAQs**, as they are called, are usually posted to the group once every three to four weeks so that new users can find them. You may want to hold off asking a question to a group until you have read its FAQ.

RESPONDING TO AN ARTICLE

If you've just read an article to which you really want to respond, you can send a private message to the author of the article or post a response to the newsgroup.

BOX 3.2

JUST THE FAQs, JACK

Newsgroups have a curious phenomenon associated with them. It turns out that, as new groups of people discover a newsgroup and join it, they will invariably start out by asking the same set of questions that the last group of people to join the newsgroup asked. Instead of answering these questions again and again, the long-term subscribers of a newsgroup often put together a "Frequently Asked Questions" list, or FAQ.

Even though FAQs are put together by volunteers, they are almost always a rich source of (usually) valid information. There is no way of guaranteeing the authority of the answers in FAQs, but consider this—if anyone does supply the wrong answer for a frequently asked question, several other people will usually supply the right answer.

If you are looking for basic information on a particular subject, you may want to invest some time in finding the newsgroup FAQ that deals with that subject. Usually the FAQ is posted every few weeks on a newsgroup.

Also, FAQs are archived at the FTP sites, such as rtfm.mit.edu and pit-manager.mit.edu. FTP is discussed in Chapter 6, along with specific examples involving retrieving FAQs. Another source of FAQs is through the WAIS index usenet.src, which indexes all the FAQs stored at pit-manager.mit.edu.

There is one thing you need to remember as you send a reply. The WinVN program automatically inserts the sender's address—your address. The address it uses is the one that you indicated when you installed the WinVN program. So, if you are using your friend's computer to read the news, you should be careful before sending a response to a news article, as your friend's e-mail address will appear as the sender.

✦ To post your response on the newsgroup, have the article displayed on the screen, then from the <u>R</u>espond menu, select Fo<u>l</u>lowup Article or press CTRL-**L**.

✦ To e-mail your response to the original poster, have the article displayed onscreen, then from the <u>R</u>espond menu, select F<u>o</u>llowup Mail or press CTRL-**O**.

In either case, the **Followup window**, similar to the one shown in Figure 3.8 is displayed. Notice that the To and Subject fields are already filled and that the original article is already included in the message section, with a > mark in front of each line. You can edit the article to insert your message. When you are ready to send the message, open the <u>P</u>ost (Followup Article) or the <u>M</u>ail (Followup Mail) menu and select <u>S</u>end.

NOTE: If you find an article you'd like to send to a friend (forward), then open the <u>R</u>espond menu and select <u>F</u>orward Article or press CTRL-**B**.

FIGURE 3.8

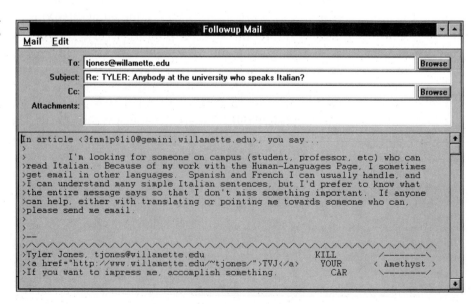

Don't follow up with a posting to the newsgroup unless you have something to say that would be valuable to all readers; reply to the original author instead. As you prepare a response, make sure to edit (trim down) the original article text so that only the parts you are responding to are included.

UNSUBSCRIBING TO A NEWSGROUP

You may decide after a while that you no longer want to regularly read a newsgroup. You can **unsubscribe**. Remember, unsubscribing does not mean you cannot read the newsgroup ever again. You can find it in the unsubscribed group list, and can resubscribe later.

To unsubscribe a newsgroup, select it in the Main Group-List window. Then from the Group menu, select Unsubscribe Selected Groups.

 Be sure to quit the WinVN program.

Just one last word of warning about newsgroups. As with all of the communication tools we've looked at so far (e-mail, listservs, and Usenet), it is important to be aware that your message can end up in some surprising places. Never send anything that you wouldn't want the world to see. In general, the Internet is a friendly place with lots of people ready to help each other with problems, questions, and conversation, and it is up to us to keep it that way.

SUMMARY

In this chapter, many of the terms and concepts that are necessary for you to read Usenet news are introduced:

✦ Usenet is a collection of thousands of topically organized newsgroups.

✦ Newsgroups are a forum for free expression; no one controls or regulates the groups.

✦ News articles are received through news feeds. A news administrator at each site determines which newsgroups are received.

✦ Newsgroups are organized into categories, as described by the first word of the newsgroup name.

✦ News reader programs help keep track of news items you have already seen and display new news and newsgroups as they appear. They also let you respond to articles by either sending e-mail to the person who posted the article or to the entire newsgroup.

KEY TERMS

articles	netnews	postings
FAQ	news	subscribe
Followup window	news administrator	threads
Main group-list window	news feed	unsubscribe
moderator	newsgroups	Usenet

REVIEW QUESTIONS

1. What is a newsgroup?

2. How does a newsgroup differ from a listserv?

3. Who controls newsgroups?

4. What does a news administrator do?

5. How are newsgroups organized?

6. In WinVN, what does it mean to subscribe to a newsgroup?

7. In WinVN, how would you go about finding a newsgroup dealing with Japanese culture?

8. In WinVN, can you read a newsgroup to which you have not subscribed? Explain.

9. In WinVN, what options do you have for responding to a newsgroup article?

10. What is a thread? How do you display or read all articles in a thread?

EXERCISES

1. Go to the misc.test newsgroup. Read the articles and submit a follow-up posting.

2. Find the names of two newsgroups on the topic of education. Describe them.

3. You've heard that there are some newsgroups especially established for questions and answers about the different "hierarchies." Find and read postings to these newsgroups and describe their contents.

4. Find a discussion group about some aspect of your ethnic background or a culture that interests you. What is the name of the newsgroup? Discuss some interesting postings.

5. Find any newsgroups that are primarily in languages other than English. Name the newsgroup and the language used.

DISCUSSION TOPICS

1. Your instructor is interested in continuing classroom discussion on the 'net. Between listservs and newsgroups, what are the advantages of one over the other?

2. Is Usenet a valid resource for information? How would you use it?

GOPHER AND VERONICA
What's on the Menu?

C H A P T E R

4

OBJECTIVES

Upon completing the material presented in this chapter, you should understand the following aspects of the Internet:

◆ The concept behind Gopher

◆ How to use Gopher

◆ How to start a Gopher client

◆ How to navigate through Gopher menus

◆ Strategies for browsing the Internet via Gopher

◆ The effective use of subject trees

◆ How to use Veronica to search for resources

BEFORE YOU START

In order to perform online exercises in this chapter, you need the following:

◆ An IBM PC compatible running Windows and connected to the Internet

◆ An installed copy of the WSGopher software on the PC that you are using. The version shown here is WS Gopher 1.2.

WHAT'S A GOPHER?

Gopher is a consistent, menu-driven interface that allows users to access a large number of varied resources on the Internet without requiring users to know a lot of arcane computer commands. With Gopher, accessing information on the Internet can be as easy as making a selection on a menu. No matter where you are on the Internet, the interface is always the same. It allows users to locate, see, and retrieve information throughout the Internet as if it were in folders and menus on their computer. Anyone can make use of the resources available on the Internet by using Gopher.

The Internet is a powerful communication tool that allows people to cooperate over distances. Even if this were all that the Internet had to offer, it would still be a tremendous tool to bring us together as communities and create opportunities for collaborative work. The Internet is also a repository of vast storage houses of digital information. Computers are, after all, tireless beasts that will answer our whims quickly, even late at night, without citing such excuses as "I've got other projects to do," or "I've got to sleep." Why not, then, entrust databases of information to computers, and allow them to serve people's requests for information? Especially if the information is to be publicly available, it makes sense to do just that, and Gopher is a tool by which this is made possible.

Gopher was developed by a team of programmers at the University of Minnesota and was released in April of 1991. It allowed campus computer users to quickly gain access to information available on their campus computer network. Within the space of a year, however, Gopher began to catch on in popularity both as a means of making information available and for accessing information. Within two years, there were more than 2,000 registered Gopher servers, computer sites where information is made available through the use of Gopher, and doubtless hundreds more that were unregistered or experimental.

Menu choices available on a Gopher server include text files, graphic images, sounds, or even another menu. These resources may reside on the current computer system (whose menu you are viewing) or on a completely different system, perhaps on the other side of the world! **GopherSpace**, the term used to refer to all the menus and information accessible through the use of Gopher, is a tree-like structure: There is a root server (menu) from which you start, and as you go up the tree into the structure, branches (other menus) will shoot off in every direction. In a properly maintained Gopher server, however, this tree will be well-organized by subject matter, making navigation easy.

| NOTE: | Depending on the computer system you are using to access Gopher, you may not be able to display or utilize retrieved information. For example, you cannot display a graphic image or play audio files unless the equipment you are using has the capability to do so. |

There are two major types of Gopher servers: the Campus Wide Information System (CWIS) and the general audience information server.

✦ A **CWIS** generally contains information of interest to the students, faculty, and staff of a particular school or organization. In addition to the campus-related information, such as campus events and course information, it often contains pointers to other Gopher sites including general audience information servers or Gopher-available information of particular interest to the campus community.

✦ A general audience information server is devoted to providing specific kinds of information that will be of use to large groups of people—for example, the lyrics server at University of Wisconsin (Parkside), weather forecasts, or archives of mailing lists and newsgroups.

HOW DOES IT WORK?

Gopher is based on what is called a *client/server* architecture. There is a Gopher client program and a Gopher server program. The **Gopher server** program runs on those host computers that are Gopher servers—information providers. The server program sits around and waits for clients to ask it about menus and documents. Whenever it is asked about any such item, it graciously provides it to the client, and then returns to its slumber. A user runs the **Gopher client** program to access information on the Gopher server. The client program takes the user's keystrokes, displays menus, retrieves and displays documents, and performs all the oddments that don't require the machine on the far side of the network.

The only impact this architecture has on you, however, is that sometimes you may find certain documents or menus take a long time to show up on-screen, or refuse to show up at all. This is because, as you wander through GopherSpace, you will probably interact with several different servers, even though you will still be using the same client. Sometimes these servers are extremely popular, or have a slow network connection, or perhaps have simply gone down for one of the many reasons that computers do. But don't lose heart! In the face of these difficulties, one can always back up and try a different approach to accessing the same information. In GopherSpace, many tunnels lead to the same information.

Rather than talk any more about Gopher, let's dive right in. We won't need a wet suit, because GopherSpace is a more-or-less friendly, warm ocean in which to swim. There are five basic steps you need to know: (1) how to start Gopher; (2) how to specify the Gopher server you want to access; (3) how to navigate through the Gopher menus; (4) how to make a selection; and (5) how to get off.

GETTING ON AND OFF

The first step is to invoke the Gopher—you need to run a Gopher client program. The client program may reside on your Windows computer, a Windows server, or on a mainframe. Here, a Gopher client, WSGopher, on a Windows computer is used.

 Visually locate the WSGopher icon in the Program Manager window. It should look similar to the one shown below:

Gopher

To start the WSGopher program, double-click on the WSGopher icon.

A screen similar to the one shown in Figure 4.1 is displayed.

Quitting the session is done as with many other Windows applications.

Double-click on the Control-menu box at the top left corner.

The session ends.

If you also want to quit WSGopher, you can open the File menu and select Exit. Leave the software running for the time being.

How the Gopher host menu displays depends on how the client software was installed. If your site is running a Gopher server, the menu displayed by the client will most likely be the menu from that server. Otherwise, it will present you with the main menu from another server which will (hopefully) provide a good starting place from which you may find information.

FIGURE 4.1

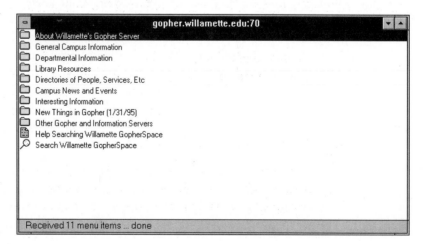

Because Gopher was developed at the University of Minnesota, the default setting for Gopher clients is often the menu from the University of Minnesota. The Minnesota Gopher screen is shown in Figure 4.3. The one in Figure 4.1 is

---

BOX 4.1

I CAN'T GET NO

I can't get no/ Gopher connection!/
I can't get no/ interaction!/
And I try, and I try, and I try, and I try . . .

Normally, your request to connect to a Gopher should go through without a hitch, and the Gopher menu should display for you. Occasionally, because the Internet is the kind of place that it is, connections don't work, and the Gopher client will display (sometimes cryptic) error messages.

Connection refused	For some reason, the Gopher server machine to which you are trying to connect is not answering or cannot answer requests. The system may be down for repairs, or overloaded, or down for some other reason.
Hostname lookup failure	It may be that the machine you've asked for no longer exists or that you didn't properly enter the name of the machine (if you were in fact typing it in). Sometimes for no apparent reason, you'll get this error message.
Connection timed out	Here, there was some problem with connecting to the remote Gopher machine. Your client waited for information to come back as long as it could, but for some reason, it was not forthcoming from the other end.
File *<filename>* not found, or or 0-Cannot access directory '/*name*/ ' error.host	Sometimes Gopher information is moved or removed, yet old menus still refer to it. If you receive this type of error message, you must look for the information elsewhere.

These errors are not catastrophes. They may mean that you have to try again later (when the remote machine is functioning again) or find some other Gopher site that has the information you desire. As you will see, many tunnels through GopherSpace lead to the same destination.

BOX 4.2

GOPHER CLIENTS ON OTHER PLATFORMS

Gopher clients are available on various platforms, such as Gopher on UNIX, TurboGopher for Macintosh, and WinSock Gopher for Microsoft Windows. Each client takes the flavor of the platform on which it's running. For example, to run the Windows Gopher program, double-click on the Gopher icon. To make a selection, double-click with the mouse or use the (ENTER) key; to close a menu, double-click on the close box in the upper left corner. Using the Windows client is like doing anything else in Windows. The same is true with the Macintosh version. The UNIX version requires that you type in the command using keystrokes. Although the interfaces may vary, almost anything that you can do on one Gopher client, you can do on another.

from Willamette University. Notice that they are very similar. You will find the similarity in all Gopher menus, thus the consistency.

For the purpose of the exercises presented here, you will access the Gopher at the University of Minnesota; from there, you will navigate through the Internet Gopher structure to the Willamette University Gopher. You may have already accessed the Minnesota Gopher in the previous section, but you will do so again in a slightly different way.

GOING DOWN TO MINNESOTA

Gopher clients generally allow you to connect directly to Gophers other than your local Gopher (the one already preset by the client software) by specifying the name of the desired Gopher computer. With WSGopher, you can connect to another Gopher by opening the File menu and selecting the New Gopher Item option or pressing (CTRL)-**N** (hold down the (CTRL) key and press **N**).

 From the File menu, select New Gopher Item or press (CTRL)-**N**.

The Fetch this Gopher Item dialog box, similar to the one shown in Figure 4.2, is displayed.

In the Server name field, type the address of the Gopher to which you wish to connect. For example, the Gopher server at Willamette University has the address of gopher.willamette.edu. In addition, you may or may not need to specify the **port** in the Server port field. The port refers to a specific communication channel on which the destination Gopher server is waiting for requests (similar to a phone extension). The standard port is 70, but sometimes a Gopher server uses a nonstandard port number. If so, change the entry to the alternate port number. In general, if you do not know the port number, you can assume 70.

FIGURE 4.2

Fetch this Gopher Item
Title:
Server name:
Server port:
70
Selector:
Item type:
Directory
Gopher+
Ask form
URL:
Paste
OK
Cancel
Help

Gopher.micro.umn.edu is the address for the Gopher server at the University of Minnesota , and it is on port 70.

Start the WSGopher program, if necessary.

From the File menu, select New Gopher Item, or press CTRL-**N**.

In the Server name field, enter **gopher.micro.umn.edu**.

Make sure that the port field contains **70**.

Click on OK or press ENTER.

The University of Minnesota root menu appears, similar to the one shown in Figure 4.3.

THE GOPHER MENU

Types of information provided are mostly either information relevant to the campus itself or collections of information available elsewhere on the Internet. Note that this is the **root Gopher server**—a place where you start the search for

FIGURE 4.3

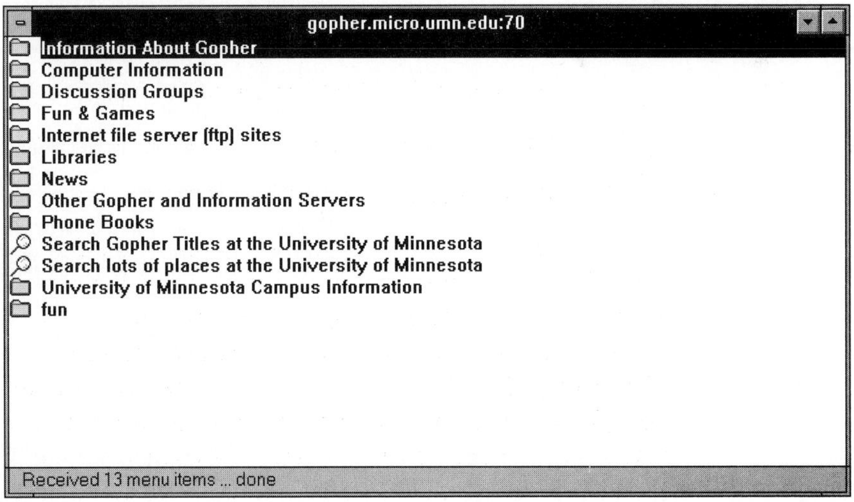
gopher.micro.umn.edu:70
Information About Gopher
Computer Information
Discussion Groups
Fun & Games
Internet file server (ftp) sites
Libraries
News
Other Gopher and Information Servers
Phone Books
Search Gopher Titles at the University of Minnesota
Search lots of places at the University of Minnesota
University of Minnesota Campus Information
fun
Received 13 menu items ... done

information. It is the top menu level on the particular Gopher server which you are using. The appearance of the menu and the way in which you make selections will depend on the platform you are using. Nevertheless, the idea is that you start from the root menu, follow the structure by making menu selections, and eventually end up with the information for which you are looking. Search tools can help you get to the resource without getting lost in GopherSpace.

On the menu, the type of selection is indicated. In the Windows platform, icons that precede menu options indicate the selection type. Table 4.1 shows the symbols and their meanings.

NOTE: For information on uncompressing PC files, see Chapter 6, FTP, Box 6.1.

TABLE 4.1   MENU OPTION ICONS

ICON	SELECTION TYPE	EXPLANATION
🖹	A file; text to be viewed	A file that can be displayed by nearly every kind of computer. The text is not formatted as it may be on a word processor. The file can be displayed on the screen, then saved, e-mailed to yourself, or printed.
🗁	A directory	When you select this item, another menu is displayed.
🔍	A searchable index	A collection of documents that has been fully indexed by every word contained within them. When you select this menu item, you are asked for a word on which to search the index.
TEL	Launches a Telnet session	When you make this selection, you will leave the Gopher program to access a remote computer system. The Gopher client will present a warning as well as information on how to get into and out of the system to which you've telnetted.
☎	A directory search service	Displays name, phone numbers, e-mail, and mailing address of the person for whom you are searching.
BH	A Mac binary file	A Macintosh "binhex" file; can only be used on a Mac.
DOS	A DOS file	A DOS archive of some sort.
10 011	A binary file	Binary code cannot be viewed. It can be saved.
▨	A graphics file	Pictures in various formats, such as GIF. Not all clients can handle this information.
🔊	Digitized sound	Not all clients can handle this information.
☹	Error	Server returned an error. Most likely when a Veronica server is too busy or a Gopher directory is under construction.
?	Unknown file type	WSGopher did not recognize this Gopher type.

BROWSING GOPHERSPACE

When **browsing** through GopherSpace, you make a selection and see what options are displayed next, make another selection and see what happens, and so on, until you find that piece of information that is of interest to you. You discover the menus that someone else has (hopefully) thoughtfully designed to present information. Unlike other Internet tools, when you use Gopher, you gain a certain sense of places within the Internet: From the University of Minnesota Gopher, choose Other Gopher and Information Services, then North America, and so on. There is often logic and organization to individual menu structures used in Gopher, but for the most part you are exploring the links that connect Gophers and resources, creating your own structure or trail as you go.

With the exercises and examples that follow, you will learn how to select and navigate effectively in this virtual metropolis. The best way to become familiar with Gopher is to use it persistently. Later in this chapter, you will learn how to use search tools available on Gopher so that you are not just blindly looking for information.

To give an idea of how Gopher can be used to accomplish a specific research task, you will use the browse method to find the Gopher at Willamette University.

In the menu display, as shown in Figure 4.3, you can select an entry by clicking on it. Pressing (ENTER) after selecting an entry, or double-clicking on an entry, will cause WSGopher to try to connect you to that resource. Other commands are available via the pull-down menus in the menu bar. You will learn more about this during the hands-on exercises.

 Select the Other Gopher and Information Servers option by using one of the methods previously described.

The Other Gopher and Information Servers menu is displayed.

You have just opened a menu and moved further into GopherSpace! The screen now displays a list of Gophers or information servers that you can access, by geographic location or by type of server.

 Select and open All the Gopher Servers in the World.

There may be a considerable pause, then a new menu appears, similar to the one shown in Figure 4.4.

This menu displays a list of all officially announced Gopher hosts in the world. In the Windows platform as shown in Figure 4.4, a scrollbar on the right allows you to scroll through the list. Currently there are over 2,300 Gophers listed in this section (and these are only the officially announced Gophers; many

FIGURE 4.4

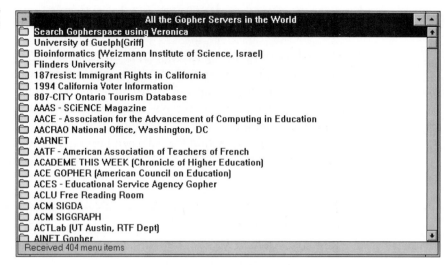

unannounced Gophers lurk deep in GopherSpace for discovery). Undoubtedly, by the time you are using this book, the number will have increased.

Perhaps you may want to go back to the previous menu so that you can pursue another menu option. You can get a list of previous menus, or places you've connected before, from the Window menu.

Open the Window menu.

A list of resources to which you have connected previously will appear similar to the one shown in Figure 4.5.

Select Other Gopher and Information Servers.

The Other Gopher and Information Servers window is displayed again.

NOTE: You could also click on the Back track button (⊞) to get back one menu level.

FIGURE 4.5

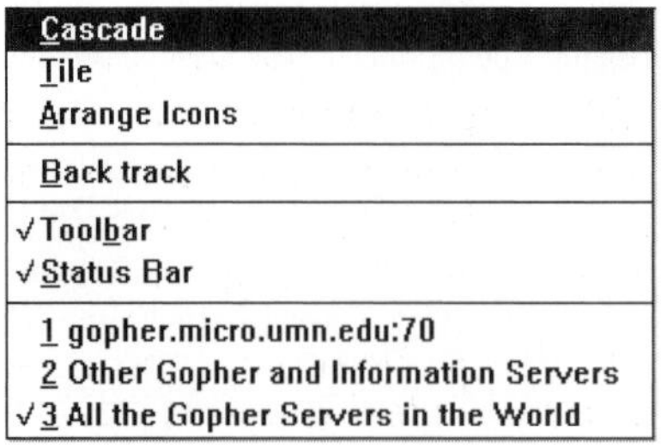

Cascade
Tile
Arrange Icons
Back track
√ Toolbar
√ Status Bar
1 gopher.micro.umn.edu:70
2 Other Gopher and Information Servers
√ 3 All the Gopher Servers in the World

Perhaps the most important command you can know in Gopher, or indeed any computer program, is how to get help. To get help, open the <u>H</u>elp menu from the menu bar. The WSGopher help is similar to Help in other MS Windows applications. You can use the <u>I</u>ndex option to search for the topic in which you are interested or you could select <u>C</u>ontext help, which allows you to point to an item onscreen and get help on that item.

Right now, you will look for the Gopher at Willamette University in Oregon. You can see that the currently displayed menu is organized by geographical location. Hence, you should not have much trouble locating the Gopher at Willamette.

 Make sure that the Other Gopher and Information Servers menu is displayed, and select the North America option.

You should see a menu listing countries or territories that have Gopher servers officially announced. USA should be one of them.

Select the USA option.

The USA menu should appear, listing all the states alphabetically. A directory at the top is labelled All; it lists all United States Gophers.

Scroll the screen to locate Oregon and select it.

A menu of Oregon Gophers should open.

Find and select the Willamette University Gopher.

The main menu of the Willamette Gopher, as was shown in Figure 4.1, is displayed.

You have swum through the seas of information to get to a goal, a particular Gopher server somewhere on the Internet.

CAMPUS WIDE INFORMATION SYSTEM

The Willamette University Gopher is an example of a Campus Wide Information System (CWIS). Many colleges and universities have adopted Gopher as a tool to disseminate information about the campus. As you saw in Figure 4.1, several menu options exist for publicizing campus information. If you are looking for information about a college or a university, you can go through the All the Gophers in the World option to see if there is a CWIS for the institution.

Many CWISs also include a directory of faculty, staff, and students, often called a **phone book**, and list their e-mail addresses. If you are looking for the e-mail address of someone at a particular institution, again locate the Gopher and see if there is such a directory service.

BOX 4.3	## BOOKMARKS

One thing about Gopher is that it is easy to get lost in GopherSpace, and sometimes laborious to retrace the route that has brought you to useful information or an intriguing resource. It would be handy to be able to keep track of these places, so that finding them again is easy to do. **Bookmarks** are for just that. They are the method by which the client allows you to mark useful spots for later reference.

You can add any type of item to your bookmark list, including directories or the results of searches. You can easily add whole categories of information. Your bookmark list will appear as a menu, and you can select items from it. In this way you can create your own hierarchical menu of Gopher sites that you visit frequently.

You may discover that many bookmarks have already been created. You can see them by opening the <u>B</u>ookmark menu and selecting <u>F</u>etch or clicking on the Fetch button (). Bookmarks may be arranged in categories. Category names are listed in the left-hand box, and as you select various categories, individual items in those categories are listed on the right.

To make a bookmark,

Select a menu item.

From the <u>B</u>ookmark menu, select <u>A</u>dd Bookmark or click on the Add Bookmark button ().

The Select category to save bookmark in dialog box is displayed as shown below.

Select a category and click OK.

You can also edit bookmarks at any time by opening the <u>B</u>ookmark menu and selecting Edit Bookmarks or by clicking on the Edit Bookmarks button ().

SUBJECT TREES

Browsing through GopherSpace is easy. You explore just by selecting those items on the menu that look interesting. Sometimes you end up with some interesting results. But what about more sophisticated usage of Gopher? What if you don't want to just browse, relying solely on serendipity to bring you the information you seek?

Some Gophers are organized in such a way to make it easier for you to find resources for a specific topic. Although it is true that all Gopher menus are somewhat organized by subject, some sites have invested a lot of time and effort in creating menus and organizations that make locating resources on the Internet easier. Such sites are said to have a **subject tree.** You will find these on menu options under a variety of names: subject resources, study carrels, topical resources, Internet Resources by Subject, and so on. All of these indicate an arrangement of resources by some subject scheme.

The Willamette University Library Gopher has such an organization. Let's say that you were given the following assignment: Find documents pertaining to the U.S. federal budget.

 From the main menu of the Willamette Gopher, select Library Resources.

A menu, similar to the one shown in Figure 4.6, appears.

Listed on the Willamette University Library Gopher menu are directories for different Internet services, analogous to what you would find in a library. The Hatfield Library Online Catalog connects you to the online catalog of the library

FIGURE 4.6

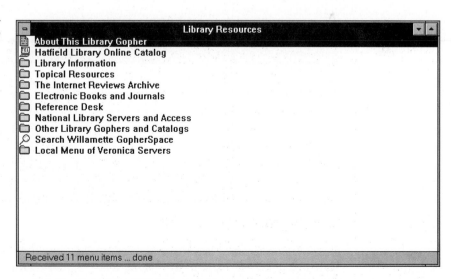

to search the book collection. The Reference Desk contains resources that provide often-used or general reference information, such as dictionaries, indexes to information, and other reference tools. The Other Library Gophers and Catalogs and Library of Congress Catalog and Gopher give access to other library information systems for perusing their online catalogs, and other resources not to be found at Willamette. Finally, the Topical Resources option is the subject tree of this Gopher, where resources are organized by subject. Here, search the Topical Resources menu for economics resources and leave these other menus for later exploration.

 Select Topical Resources.

A menu similar to the one shown in Figure 4.7 is displayed.

NOTE: As your screen begins to clutter with a lot of opened windows, you can maximize the current window so that other windows are not visible.

Here, you see one example of a subject scheme: The designers of this Gopher have attempted to classify information by subject. Initial options are very general, leading to more specific categories, such as Psychology, Sociology, and Education. Management and Business Economics seems to be a good place to start looking for information on the federal budget.

 Select Management and Business Economics.

The menu again offers further options.

FIGURE 4.7

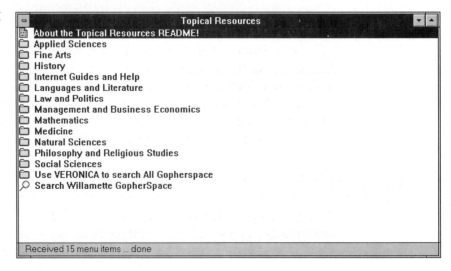

BOX 4.4

WELL-CONSTRUCTED SUBJECT TREES

Here is a list of a few Gophers with good subject trees that you may want to try. To connect directly, specify the address. For example, to connect to North Carolina State University, open the File menu and select New Gopher Item or press (CTRL)-**N**. Then enter **dewey.lib.ncsu.edu** in the Server name field and **70** in the port field.

Library of Congress Marvel Gopher   marvel.loc.gov
  Look in the "Global Electronic Library" folder.

North Carolina State University   dewey.lib.ncsu.edu
  Look in the NCSU's "library without walls" folder
  for "Study Carrels."

RiceInfo   riceinfo.rice.edu
  Look in the "Information by Subject Area" folder.

For a collection of sites that have subject trees, try connecting to:

Michigan State University List of Subject Trees   burrow.cl.msu.edu
  Look in the "Network & Database Resources"
  folder for "Internet Resources by Subject."

The option leads you to other resources on the Internet that relate to Business and Economics. The logical place to find the information you seek seems to be Documents and Archives.

 Select Documents and Archives.

You will probably see some kind of entry for the U.S. budget.

Keep on following the tree, making selections. If you get to a dead end, back up and try another path. Eventually you will end up with a document. Once you locate a document of interest, you can view it onscreen or save the document as a file on your local computer, where you can edit and print it as any other text document. You can save the document by opening the File menu and selecting the Save Item command. A dialog box is displayed in which you can specify the location where you want the document saved.

USING SEARCH TOOLS

Subject trees provide a good "table of contents" functionality. You can browse specific subject areas to find general information on the topic. However, what if you are looking for specific information but don't know exactly where it might be located? In a book, you would use an index for such a task, and it would be useful to be able to do the same kind of thing here.

The folks at University of Nevada, Reno thought the same thing, and in the fall of 1992 they released a program that would search through GopherSpace and index all of the titles it saw. They named their program **Veronica**, an acronym for Very Easy Rodent-Oriented Net-wide Index to Computerized Archives (and to inflict a wily pun, because there already is another search program called Archie).

Veronica has two portions: One half combs the network, maintaining (somewhere between weekly and biweekly) an index of all titles of all documents on most Gopher servers—at least, registered Gopher servers. The other half of

---

BOX 4.5	## WHAT *DOES* THE 🔎 MEAN?

Often, in searching GopherSpace, you come across menu items that are searchable indexes. These items are marked with a 🔎. Beware—not all items marked as such search the same thing! In general, there are three types of searchable indexes that you will encounter, and it is important to understand the differences so that you know what you are searching.

VERONICA searches—Searches using Veronica are usually labeled as such. You can assume that a Veronica search is searching the titles of menu options in a large section of GopherSpace. Some Veronica servers may be more up to date or more inclusive than others, so it is often useful to try your search on a few different servers.

JUGHEAD or LOCAL searches—Searches labeled "Jughead" (for Jonzy's Universal Gopher Hierarchy Excavation And Display, and yes, it *is* an awful pun!) or Local search only the local menu structures. Sometimes this is a single Gopher or a group of related Gophers. For example, a menu option labeled Search Gopher Titles at the University of Minnesota would be a local search of menu items, and not as inclusive as a Veronica search. This might be useful if you are looking for materials at a local site. For example, if you were looking for the admission policy of the University of Minnesota, this would be a good search tool to use.

WAIS full text searches—These are searches of Full Text databases. They do not search Gopher titles! Often these will be labeled as: Search the Full Text of the NAFTA Agreement, or Search the Archives of This List. This can be very useful for finding material within a document or group of documents.

As always, pay attention to what type of searchable index you are using, and use one that matches your search needs.

Veronica takes requests on keywords and returns a menu of document titles (or menu titles) that contain those keywords.

First, you need to find a Veronica server.

 Back up to the Other Gopher and Information Servers menu by using the pull-down menu under <u>W</u>indow. If you do not see this item on the menu, select <u>M</u>ore Windows… to list other previously accessed locations.

A menu similar to the one in Figure 4.8 is displayed.

One of the top few options should be Veronica.

 Select Search titles in Gopherspace using veronica.

A menu similar to the one in Figure 4.9 is displayed.

FIGURE 4.8

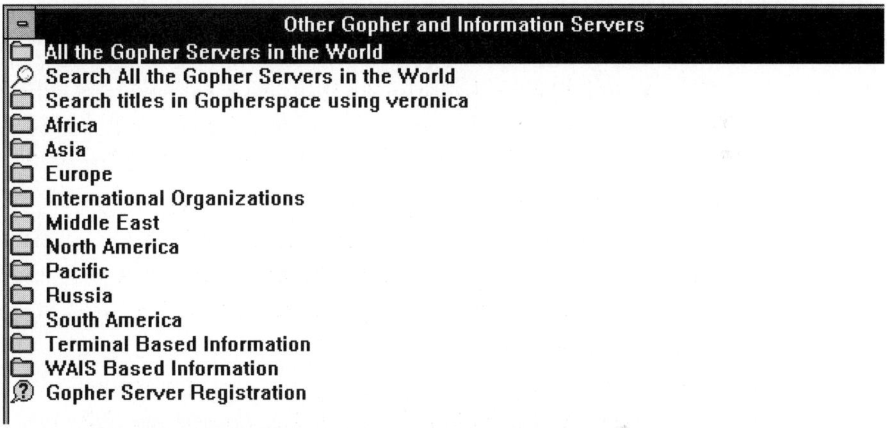

Other Gopher and Information Servers
📁 All the Gopher Servers in the World
🔎 Search All the Gopher Servers in the World
📁 Search titles in Gopherspace using veronica
📁 Africa
📁 Asia
📁 Europe
📁 International Organizations
📁 Middle East
📁 North America
📁 Pacific
📁 Russia
📁 South America
📁 Terminal Based Information
📁 WAIS Based Information
❓ Gopher Server Registration

FIGURE 4.9

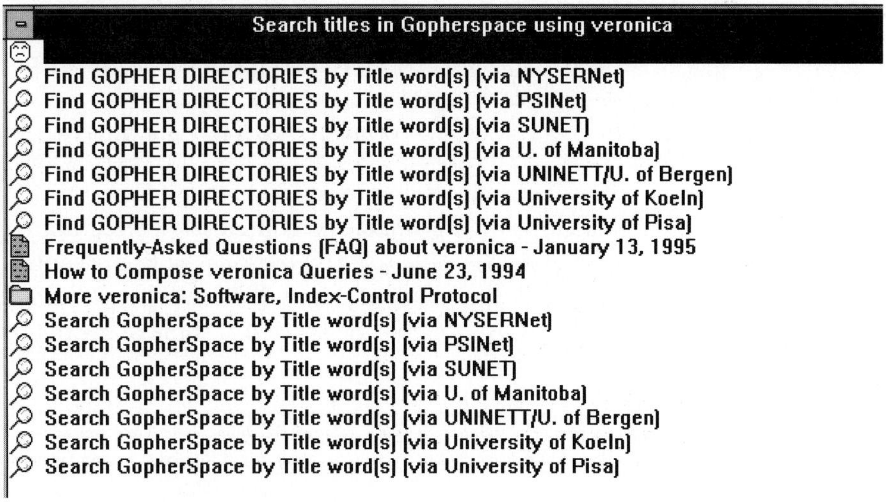

Search titles in Gopherspace using veronica
🔎 Find GOPHER DIRECTORIES by Title word(s) (via NYSERNet)
🔎 Find GOPHER DIRECTORIES by Title word(s) (via PSINet)
🔎 Find GOPHER DIRECTORIES by Title word(s) (via SUNET)
🔎 Find GOPHER DIRECTORIES by Title word(s) (via U. of Manitoba)
🔎 Find GOPHER DIRECTORIES by Title word(s) (via UNINETT/U. of Bergen)
🔎 Find GOPHER DIRECTORIES by Title word(s) (via University of Koeln)
🔎 Find GOPHER DIRECTORIES by Title word(s) (via University of Pisa)
📄 Frequently-Asked Questions (FAQ) about veronica - January 13, 1995
📄 How to Compose veronica Queries - June 23, 1994
📁 More veronica: Software, Index-Control Protocol
🔎 Search GopherSpace by Title word(s) (via NYSERNet)
🔎 Search GopherSpace by Title word(s) (via PSINet)
🔎 Search GopherSpace by Title word(s) (via SUNET)
🔎 Search GopherSpace by Title word(s) (via U. of Manitoba)
🔎 Search GopherSpace by Title word(s) (via UNINETT/U. of Bergen)
🔎 Search GopherSpace by Title word(s) (via University of Koeln)
🔎 Search GopherSpace by Title word(s) (via University of Pisa)

Some of the items are help files, readable just as any other Gopher text file. There may be information there about new features or services of Veronica. You can read these to learn more about Veronica and how to compose search queries. Other menu options come in two categories:

◆ Find GOPHER DIRECTORIES by Title words(s)... will accept **keywords** to search only *titles of folders* in GopherSpace. It *ignores* all other Gopher items.

◆ Search GopherSpace by Title word(s)... will accept keywords you enter to search all the Gopher titles about which the Veronica server knows. This includes any directory, file, search tools, sound file, or telnet session. If your keyword matches any item at all, the item will be returned to you on a menu.

NOTE: There are several Veronica servers on the Internet and, hence, multiple entries in each category. Even then, there are not enough servers. Users often receive the message "Too many connections—Try again soon."

How do the two search methods differ? To find out, let's do a simple Veronica search. Different options within each category list different servers—different computers that are running the Veronica index program. If you have problems getting connected to one (which happens sometimes), try another server.

Select the Search GopherSpace by Title word(s) option.

A dialog box appears, prompting you for keywords.

You are still looking for more information on the U.S. budget.

Type **budget** and press ⒠ⓃⓉⒺⓇ or click the Search button.

A brief pause should ensue. During this time, your Gopher client should assure you that it is performing various tasks by displaying messages in the status bar across the bottom of the screen. Messages that appear are: "connecting," "waiting for response," and "receiving response." As long as you see one of these status messages, you can be assured that your Gopher client is still at work for you.

A new menu should appear, similar to the one shown in Figure 4.10.

If your client is unable to connect for some reason, it will report so on the status line. If you are unable to connect, try selecting one of the other Search GopherSpace by Title word(s) options. Not only should your screen be full of options, but the entire menu itself should be inordinately long. As you scroll through the list, you may be amazed at some of the options. The information located includes the following:

◆ Reviews of books or other documents

◆ Brief references or annotations to documents not present

FIGURE 4.10

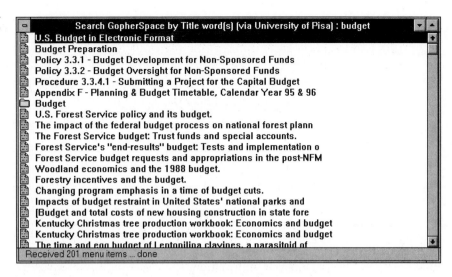

Search GopherSpace by Title word(s) (via University of Pisa) : budget
- U.S. Budget in Electronic Format
- Budget Preparation
- Policy 3.3.1 - Budget Development for Non-Sponsored Funds
- Policy 3.3.2 - Budget Oversight for Non-Sponsored Funds
- Procedure 3.3.4.1 - Submitting a Project for the Capital Budget
- Appendix F - Planning & Budget Timetable, Calendar Year 95 & 96
- Budget
- U.S. Forest Service policy and its budget.
- The impact of the federal budget process on national forest plann
- The Forest Service budget: Trust funds and special accounts.
- Forest Service's "end-results" budget: Tests and implementation o
- Forest Service budget requests and appropriations in the post-NFM
- Woodland economics and the 1988 budget.
- Forestry incentives and the budget.
- Changing program emphasis in a time of budget cuts.
- Impacts of budget restraint in United States' national parks and
- [Budget and total costs of new housing construction in state fore
- Kentucky Christmas tree production workbook: Economics and budget
- Kentucky Christmas tree production workbook: Economics and budget
- The time and egg budget of Leptopilina clavines, a parasitoid of

Received 201 menu items ... done

BOX 4.6

BOOLEAN SEARCH

Veronica has one additional feature that is important, as it reappears on the Internet and in electronic resources in general. Veronica supports Boolean operators. Boolean operators are the words AND, OR, and NOT, and you place them between keywords to expand or limit the scope of your search. When you type in more than one word for Veronica to seek, and you don't put an AND, OR, or NOT between the words, Veronica assumes AND. You could alternatively put ORs and NOTs between words.

For example, if you perform a Veronica directory title search for "dogs cats" or "dogs *and* cats," it finds all resources that have *both* "dogs" *and* "cats" in the titles. You've limited the search to title entries with both keywords. If you perform a Veronica search for "dogs *or* cats," Veronica finds those titles that contain either "dogs" *or* "cats" or both. You will find more things than if you used "and." Now, if you perform a Veronica search for "dogs *not* cats," it finds those title entries that contain only "dogs," but never with the word "cats."

You can link together keywords with more than one Boolean operator, and you can use parentheses to separate distinct units: searching for "(dogs and cats) *not* (frogs or cars)" would return titles with *both* "dogs" and "cats," *only if* those titles did not have either "frogs" or "cars."

You can get really spiffy, and define very exacting searches with Booleans and parentheses. But as far as Veronica is concerned, it usually takes more time to compose a complex search of several keywords than to type in two or three truly relevant keywords. By spending a little time to come up with clear and concise keywords, you can save a lot of time.

BOX 4.7	**OTHER NOTABLE GOPHER SITES**

The following is a list of sites you may want to try.

Resource	Address
Coalition for Networked Information	gopher.cni.org
Electronic Newsstand	gopher.enews.com
Enviromental Protection Agency Gopher	gopher.epa.gov
The Internet Society	ietf.CNRI.Reston.Va.US
MARVEL Library of Congress Gopher	marvel.loc.gov
National Science Foundation Gopher	stis.nsf.gov

Scholarly Electronic Conferences
    Look in the Computing folder for
    Internet Information.
	gopher.usask.ca 70

United Nations	nywork1.undp.org

White House Information
    Includes Press Releases—look in the fol-
    lowing folders: Browse Information by
    Subject, Government Information, and
    Information from the White House.
	gopher.tamu.edu

World Health Organization	gopher.who.ch

✦ Files that were listed but were accessible only from on-site (this means the document probably contained copyrighted or local information that the owners did not want widely available)

✦ Some actual documents that deal directly with the federal budget

Of the mixture of types of findings, you will find that the vast majority are irrelevant to your needs. Perhaps the reviews and annotations might give pointers to further resources, and perhaps a small percentage actually contain useful information. You need to sort through all the selections, but there's just so much.

This is where the Find GOPHER DIRECTORIES by Title word(s)… Veronica search comes in. If you try the same search with a directory-searching Veronica, you won't necessarily get fewer returns (although you often will), but you will gain another advantage. Your findings will consist of directories only, and a directory will contain a collection of relevant information, providing more organization to the otherwise unorganized list of sources.

Back up to the previous menu, Search titles in Gopherspace using veronica.
Select a Find GOPHER DIRECTORIES by Title word(s)... option, and enter the word **budget** as the keyword.

You should get a menu of returns, all directories, similar to the one shown in Figure 4.11.

NOTE: Depending on the site you select, you may or may not retrieve entries. If you can't connect or find any matches, try another server.

There are shortcomings to using Veronica: It searches only titles, and it has no way of knowing the content or subject of a particular file in its index. Indeed, you have no way of knowing what words are more commonly used to refer to what subjects. You need to be careful when using Veronica; have a list of synonyms and words related to the target in mind when you use it; skip irrelevant returns immediately; do not spend time chasing something that doesn't appear to be there. We are at the mercy of the people who name Gopher files when we use Veronica. Although the file names are often descriptive, we shouldn't expect too much of them.

From the File menu, select Exit or press (ALT)-**4**.

FIGURE 4.11

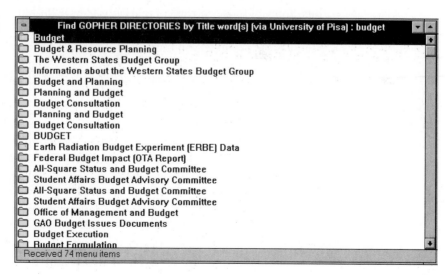

BOX 4.8 | # NO MATTER WHERE YOU GO, THERE YOU ARE . . .

Gopher is a very useful tool for finding and using information resources on the Internet. You've seen how you can search and navigate a vast area without needing to know where exactly you are going. This is great for browsing, but once you start doing research, beware! Anyone (including you) can build a Gopher for other people to use. Just because you find something in GopherSpace doesn't mean that the information is up to date or accurate. Gophers range from those that focus on particular subjects (for example, biology or government information), to large collections of various subject resources, to informational Gophers for college and university campuses. Some Gophers are updated frequently with new information (such as the White House speeches) and others have never been updated, and some just plain refuse to work. Here are some things you can do to determine what you've found.

1. Look for an entry somewhere at the top of the Gopher that has the word "about" in it. Often Gopher administrators create an "about" file to let people know what they can expect to find in that particular Gopher. Sometimes it will list the name and address of a person you can contact if you have questions, or you can try sending mail to gopher@*sitename* (the name of the site where the Gopher is located).

2. Don't trust the first answer you find to a question. Often there are many versions of resources out there in GopherSpace. For example, if you use Veronica to search for the words "electronic books," you will retrieve many hits. Some of those entries contain only a few texts, but others contain hundreds. Also, think of other words that might retrieve what you are seeking. For example, you might try "electronic texts" or "ebooks."

3. Often, you can find the same information in many different locations. Check around to see if there are multiple versions of the resource. Some sites may have full documents, and others may have only excerpts or not have any revisions. This is particularly true of text resources like government speeches or treaties. Also, you may find the resource in many different formats. For example, some sites may have it as a compressed file that you need to save and uncompress, whereas others may have it fully available and indexed!

SUMMARY

In this chapter, many of the terms and concepts that are necessary to use Gopher are introduced:

✦ A Gopher is a consistent, menu-driven interface that allows users to access information on the Internet.

✦ In order to use a Gopher, you must have access to the Gopher client program.

✦ When you start a Gopher client, a menu of the Gopher server preset by your Gopher client is displayed. However, you can specify to which Gopher server you'd like to connect.

✦ To make a selection on a Gopher menu, you can select the item and press (ENTER) or double-click on it.

✦ When you browse through GopherSpace, you make selections as they appear on the menu, depending on the organization as presented in each menu.

✦ A Campus Wide Information System (CWIS) is used by educational institutions to disseminate information about the campus. Many use Gopher as the tool.

✦ A subject tree is a Gopher menu structure where resources are presented by subject area.

✦ Veronica is a search tool within Gopher. You have the choice of doing a keyword selection to find all documents and resources or finding just directory titles containing the keyword.

KEY TERMS

bookmarks	Gopher server	root Gopher server
browsing	GopherSpace	subject tree
CWIS	keyword	Veronica
Gopher	phone book	
Gopher client	port	

REVIEW QUESTIONS

1. What is the difference between a Gopher client and a Gopher server program?

2. What is a CWIS?

3. When you run the WSGopher client program on a Windows computer, how do you specify to which Gopher server you'd like to connect?

4. How do you make selections on a Gopher menu?

5. When a Gopher menu selection runs to more than one screen, how do you view the rest of the options?

6. How do you go up a menu structure? That is, after you make a selection from a menu and decide that you want to go back to the previous menu, how do you do that?

7. Why is a subject tree useful?

8. What is Veronica?

9. In Veronica, what is the difference between Search GopherSpace by Title word(s)... and Find GOPHER DIRECTORIES by Title word(s)...?

10. How can you use Gopher to find someone's e-mail address?

EXERCISES

1. Use the Gopher tools at your disposal to find out everything you can about United States Census data.

2. Find out what the National Science Foundation has provided to the Internet community via Gopher. Specify how you found the information. List some resources found.

3. Find collections of e-journals on women's movements. Describe how you found these journals, and list where they are located.

4. Find the most up-to-date weather statistics or satellite maps for your area of the world. How far is it from your location to the nearest hurricane or tropical storm? Specify how you found your answer.

DISCUSSION TOPICS

1. What are the advantages of using Gopher? Disadvantages?

2. Assume that you are putting together an entry in a Gopher menu for your school's student government. What information should you include? How would you organize the menu structure? Would there be duplication of information or effort with other listings on Gopher?

TELNET
Warning! Leaving the Primrose Path

CHAPTER 5

OBJECTIVES

Upon completing the material presented in this chapter, you should understand the following aspects of the Internet:

✦ The concept behind Telnet

✦ How to use Telnet

✦ How to connect with other computers

✦ How to disconnect from other computers

✦ How to use Hytelnet

BEFORE YOU START

In order to perform online exercises in this chapter, you need the following:

✦ An IBM PC compatible running Windows- and connected to the Internet

✦ An installed copy of Telnet software. The software used here is Uwterm, version 0.97i.

LEAVING HOME VIA TELNET

You have used Gopher and World Wide Web elsewhere in this book to explore the Internet. With Gopher or WWW, however, you used and were forced to navigate within menus to get to where you wanted to go. However, sometimes you need to connect directly to remote resources without the aid of a menu, freeing you to explore the areas that you find interesting. This is done using a Telnet program. **Telnet** allows another computer to accept keystrokes from your keyboard and display text in a window on your PC. You may have already used Telnet to connect to your local Internet host or choose a Gopher menu item that was a Telnet resource.

Think, for a moment, what happens when you use a telephone—you pick up the receiver, enter a number, and are connected to another telephone. That phone might ring and be answered, it might give you a busy signal, or you might get a message saying that the number you have dialed is no longer in service. Telnet works much the same way, allowing you to "call" another machine and interact with whatever (or whomever!) is on the other end.

This opens up a whole world of opportunity to run programs and search databases on computers all over the world. There is a great variety of resources available to you via Telnet, ranging from simply accessing and using the computing power of another machine, to using the online catalogs of hundreds of libraries, to accessing database information services for which you must pay, to finding the NBA game schedule!

A word of warning is necessary here: Just as is leaving home in the real world, traveling by Telnet is exciting, but you must leave the familiarity of your own environment behind—once you've logged onto another machine, you are at its mercy. That remote computer can display only text, not graphics, and the mouse on your PC can be used only to cut and paste. The remote computer may offer user-friendly menus, or just a cryptic prompt awaiting your command. By paying attention to what is happening on the screen and following clues for help and instructions, you can often successfully use remote computers. Even if the remote system doesn't provide much help, you should always be able to "hang up" on that remote computer.

A second word of warning: You cannot just Telnet to any computer system you see on the Internet. Some require that you have a valid user account on their system. Some will let you connect for a specific purpose only. For example, by using the username gopher, a computer at University of Minnesota named consultant.micro.umn.edu will let you connect to use the Gopher client. Still others will let you connect and display a general menu, such as the computer named techinfo.mit.edu at MIT.

WHAT'S IN A NAME?

Just as you address an e-mail message to a user at a particular host computer, a Telnet session connects you to a specific host computer with a unique name, called the **domain name**. The address scheme for sending e-mail to a specific computer is similar to the naming scheme for computers to which you could Telnet. You would send a message to Yolanda Portofoni at Willamette University by addressing it to her e-mail address, portofon@willamette.edu; you can use the address jupiter.willamette.edu to Telnet to the Jupiter computer at Willamette University.

Each domain name is several short words separated by dots: The last word tells what kind of organization or geographical location runs the computer (for example, .com, .edu, .gov, .org, or .au for Australia). The second-to-last generally abbreviates the name of the organization or company; additional words name the subdomain, if it exists; and finally, the left-most word is the name of the computer. For example, barney.cs.indiana.edu might be the name of a machine called barney run by the Computer Science Department at Indiana University. When machines on the Internet communicate, the domain name is "looked up" and mapped to a unique number identifying the machine, called the **IP address** (typically displayed for humans as 4 numbers, each less than 256, separated by periods). As domain names are easier to remember than the IP addresses, people generally refer to a computer by its domain name. However, you can use either when using Telnet to connect to the system.

BOX 5.1

LASCIATE OGNI SPERANZA VOI CH'ENTRATE (ABANDON HOPE ALL YE WHO ENTER HERE!)

The Internet is full of mysterious sites that Telnet can access. Not only are there rich and detailed databases to search, but there are also many types of games, ranging from online versions of board games to interactive multiuser adventure games. MUDs (which stands for Multi User Dungeons) have been known to be both fascinating and incredibly addictive. To quote one player, "Beware! There seems to be a black hole of personal time that surrounds these things!" More than a few students have been devoured by these games, losing all sense of what life is like outside of the network.

Caveat emptor!

GETTING ON AND OFF

The four basic things you need to know to begin are: (1) how to start the Telnet program; (2) how to start a session with a remote computer; (3) how to end a session; and (4) how to quit the program when you are done.

Here is the scenario:

You are reading the book *Tar Baby* by Toni Morrison in your American Literature class. You enjoy this book and want to find out if she has written any other books. However, your library doesn't have any other books by her in its collection. Also, you will be writing a critical paper on her as an author, and want to track down journal literature about her.

Fortunately, Telnet can help you do this. Many library catalogs and large bibliographic databases are available via Telnet for you to use. One such database is maintained by Data Research Associates, and you decide to start there. For the moment, let's just try to get on and off the system; you will try the actual search later.

NOTE: Although this book uses the Telnet software called Uwterm, the program you use may be called "Telnet" (which would be handy) or it could be something else completely. If you can't figure out what your Telnet program is, ask your computer support staff. Whatever the software, the instructions to use the program should be very similar to the ones given here.

 Visually locate the Telnet program icon in the Program Manager window. If your Telnet program is Uwterm, it will look similar to the one shown below.

Uwterm

Start the Telnet program by double-clicking on the Telnet program icon.

The program will probably spend a little time setting up, then a dialog box similar to the one shown in Figure 5.1 will appear, prompting for a host to connect. Your software may be set up to connect to a particular host computer automatically. If so, open the Options menu and select Host/Port. The same dialog box will display.

You must specify to which computer you want to connect. As mentioned earlier, you can give either the domain name or the IP address of the system to which you want to connect. The domain name for this example is dra.com (192.65.218.43).

 In the Hostname text box, type **dra.com** and click on OK or press (ENTER).

If the connection is successful, a session window similar to the one shown in Figure 5.2 is displayed.

FIGURE 5.1

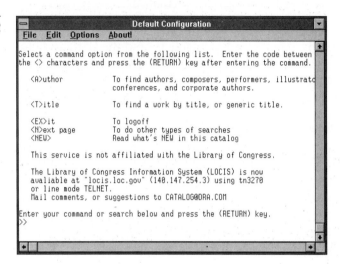

If something happened and you didn't connect, check to make sure that you typed in the name correctly. If you see the message "host unknown," most likely you have made a typing mistake. If you see some other message, it could mean that the remote machine is too busy to answer your call right now and that you should try again later. Sometimes names and addresses change with no warning, or a machine may be down, and you can't connect. This is a fact of life on the Internet, as it is with the telephone, and you have to look elsewhere for the information you seek. For the moment, let's assume that you have connected successfully.

As you can see in Figure 5.2, this system gives you a menu option to disconnect (<EX>it). However, there are many systems for which ways to disconnect are not so obvious. If you can type a command, one of the following commands may disconnect you: **logoff**, **logout**, **quit**, **bye**, **exit**. If none of this works, you always have the option to quit the Telnet program. If you need to quit the program, open the File menu and select Exit.

If you are successful at disconnecting from the remote computer, the Telnet window will close.

Type ex and press ⟨ENTER⟩.

The session window disappears.

BOX 5.2	**IS ANYBODY HOME?**

Sometimes, you cannot Telnet to a site that you visited yesterday. There are a number of causes for this quirk and often you can't do anything about it. Uwterm, the Telnet client used in writing this book, responds with a message such as "error connecting to remote host:" when it fails to make a connection. Errors can occur for the following reasons:

✦ The Telnet client is unable to find the IP address for the given domain name, either because it was entered wrong or because it doesn't exist.

✦ The remote computer is powered off, the remote computer is refusing to connect to your machine, or a computer network is down.

These are usually temporary problems. If the problem persists for more than a day, you may want to contact your local computer support staff to see if they can determine the cause. If you have the same problem with a number of different machines, you may want to contact your local computer support staff to make sure the problem is not occurring at your local site.

You've just completed a simple Telnet session. If you want to quit Telnet at this point, open the File menu and select Exit.

Now that you've successfully connected to and disconnected from a system, let's try searching that system. When connecting to remote databases, you must at least read the screens presented to you to be able to use the database. You may also find it useful to read the available help information. Some systems are easier to use than others, but it is always wise to read any information you can about the system when using it.

 Connect to the dra.com database again using the same method as earlier.

You are looking for more books by Toni Morrison.

 Type **A** for an author search and press ENTER.

The author search screen, similar to the one shown in Figure 5.3, is displayed.

You are now presented with a screen and several examples. This is why it is important to read the screen when connecting to remote systems. Although you may have never used the system before, you can often determine what to do next by reading the screen. In this case, to find books by author, type the author's name at the Enter Author prompt.

FIGURE 5.3

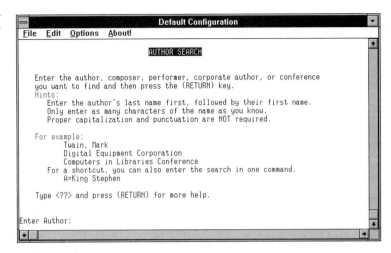

NOTE: If you make a mistake while typing, just backspace and correct your entry. If you end up somewhere you didn't intend, typing **st** should return you to the main menu.

Type **Morrison, Toni** and press ⟨ENTER⟩.

A screen similar to the one shown in Figure 5.4 is displayed.

This screen displays two sets of books. The first set contains 28 titles. To display the set, enter the line number. Right now, you want to see the first set.

Type **1** and press ⟨ENTER⟩.

A list, similar to the one shown in Figure 5.5, is displayed.

FIGURE 5.4

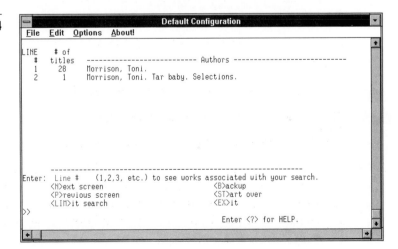

FIGURE 5.5

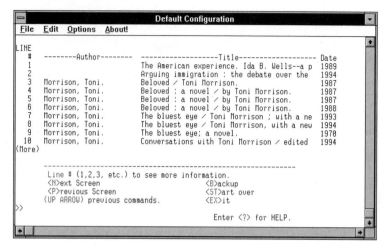

```
┌─────────────────────────  Default Configuration  ─────────────────────┐
│ File   Edit   Options   About!                                        │
├───────────────────────────────────────────────────────────────────────┤
│LINE                                                                    │
│  #    --------Author--------   ------------------Title------------------ Date
│  1                             The American experience. Ida B. Wells--a p 1989
│  2                             Arguing immigration : the debate over the  1994
│  3    Morrison, Toni.          Beloved / Toni Morrison.                   1987
│  4    Morrison, Toni.          Beloved : a novel / by Toni Morrison.      1987
│  5    Morrison, Toni.          Beloved : a novel / by Toni Morrison.      1987
│  6    Morrison, Toni.          Beloved : a novel / by Toni Morrison.      1988
│  7    Morrison, Toni.          The bluest eye / Toni Morrison ; with a ne 1993
│  8    Morrison, Toni.          The bluest eye / Toni Morrison, with a new 1994
│  9    Morrison, Toni.          The bluest eye; a novel.                   1970
│ 10    Morrison, Toni.          Conversations with Toni Morrison / edited  1994
│(More)                                                                   │
│                                                                         │
│       ----------------------------------------------------------        │
│       Line # (1,2,3, etc.) to see more information.                     │
│       <N>ext Screen                          <B>ackup                   │
│       <P>revious Screen                       <ST>art over              │
│       (UP ARROW) previous commands.           <EX>it                    │
│>>                                                                       │
│                                       Enter <?> for HELP.               │
└───────────────────────────────────────────────────────────────────────┘
```

You can see that she has written several other books. You can now decide whether you want to try to obtain one of these books through your local library or bookstore.

Now that you've found your way into the system, can you find your way back out? You have found the information you sought and need to disconnect from the session. Fortunately, there is a disconnect menu option onscreen. If, however, you don't see any obvious way to disconnect, you can try the following:

✦ Type **help** or **?** and see if anything happens. In this case, the **??** command gives you help on searching the database.

✦ Try typing **bye**, **exit**, **quit**, or **logoff**.

Type **ex** and press (ENTER).

The session window will close.

If your Telnet program is still running, open the File menu and select Exit.

USER NAMES AND TERMINAL EMULATION

As you have seen in this session, remote machines can sometimes give you very clear instructions; other times, they can be complex and confusing. Always take a look around for any help or question mark commands that you can use for further instructions on how to navigate the system to which you have connected. Take a moment now to pat yourself on the back and marvel at the fact that you've just visited a large warehouse of information without ever having left your desk.

You probably didn't notice, but in the session you just completed, several details were taken care of automatically. While this is nice, it doesn't always happen that way. Two such details were logging in and selecting a terminal emulation. Often, when you connect to a remote machine, you will be greeted by a not-so-friendly prompt: "login:". Sometimes you will know the correct way to login, and sometimes you won't. Sometimes you can guess the login name to use, because it will closely match the service you are trying to reach. For example, if you are trying to reach a library catalog, try typing the login name **library**, or if you are trying to Telnet to a Gopher, try logging in as **gopher**. You can often find a login name in the same place that you found the address. Beware: Some systems also require a password or may be restricted so that outside users cannot access them without an account. However, if you know the correct login name and still are prompted for a password, check to make sure that you have entered the login name correctly. On many systems, LIBRARY and library are considered different—that is, it matters whether you type text in upper- or lowercase characters. In most instances, lowercase is preferred.

You may now be wondering how you can find the addresses and login information of machines that might interest you. You may have noticed in Gopher that Telnet sessions were often listed. (These were the menu items with an icon of a terminal shown below.) When choosing these items from a Gopher, a dialog box will pop up to give login information such as "Use the account name 'brsuser' to log in."

The other question you are often asked upon logging in is to identify your terminal type. Just as with a telephone, you can end up calling someone who doesn't speak your language. This will appear as garbled characters on the screen. Fortunately, many systems will offer you a choice of terminal types. You may be presented with:

What kind of Terminal are you using?
     V > VT100
     W > WYSE emulating TVI925
     A > CCCII PC
     B > HEATHKIT H19
     C > TANDEM
     D > TVI910
     E > TVI920
     F > TVI925

Most Telnet software usually emulates vt100 or vt220. If, upon choosing those options, strange things happen, you may have a different type of **terminal emulation**. Ask your instructor for help.

One more piece of information that you may need when Telnetting to another machine is the port number. As mentioned in the Chapter 4, a port number is similar to a phone extension number. If you don't see any reference to a port number, you probably don't need one. However, if you do see an additional number, or port number, you can simply add it to the end of your Telnet address. For example, if you wanted to connect to the MIT MicroMuse at the address 18.43.0.102 on port number 4201, you would enter **18.43.0.102 4201** as the address when specifying the host to which you wish to connect.

HYTELNET: WHERE'S THE PHONE BOOK?

We've talked now a bit about how you can use Telnet, but we haven't told you where you can find addresses. Fortunately someone out there on the Internet has taken charge of compiling a vast database of Telnet addresses, including the addresses of most of the Internet-accessible library catalogs. The database, compiled by Peter Scott of the University of Saskatchewan, is called **Hytelnet**. You can access Hytelnet by using Telnet, Gopher (discussed in Chapter 4), or World Wide Web (discussed in Chapter 8). For now, you will use Gopher. If you have not read Chapter 4, just follow the instructions given here.

NOTE: You can Telnet to rsl.ox.ac.uk (163.1.62.31) and login as **hytelnet** to use Hytelnet. However, you will need to read the instructions on the screen very carefully. Remember, you leave the primrose path when you Telnet! Hytelnet is also available on the World Wide Web at http://www.usask.ca/cgi-bin/hytelnet.

BOX 5.3   ### THE IBM TELNET—TN3270

Although the majority of machines on the Internet allow you access through Telnet, there are a few IBM machines that talk only to a special type of terminal, a 3270. The 3270 implements a full-screen interface for IBM mainframes and uses special features. The features are so complex that you need a special version of Telnet, usually called tn3270, in order to communicate with these machines. If you have tn3270, you should be able to run it the same as Telnet. If you can't find tn3270, ask you local computer support staff for assistance.

Although Hytelnet is not a comprehensive list of every Telnet site on the Internet, it is a very good place to get an idea of the types of information and resources available. The database is frequently updated as new services become available.

Let's connect to the Hytelnet database and see what types of resources are available.

 Locate the Gopher program icon. The icon should look similar to the one below.

Gopher

Double-click on the Gopher program icon.

A screen similar to the one shown in Figure 5.6 is displayed.

From the File menu, select New Gopher Item, or press (CTRL)-N.

A dialog box similar to the one shown in Figure 5.7 is displayed.

FIGURE 5.6

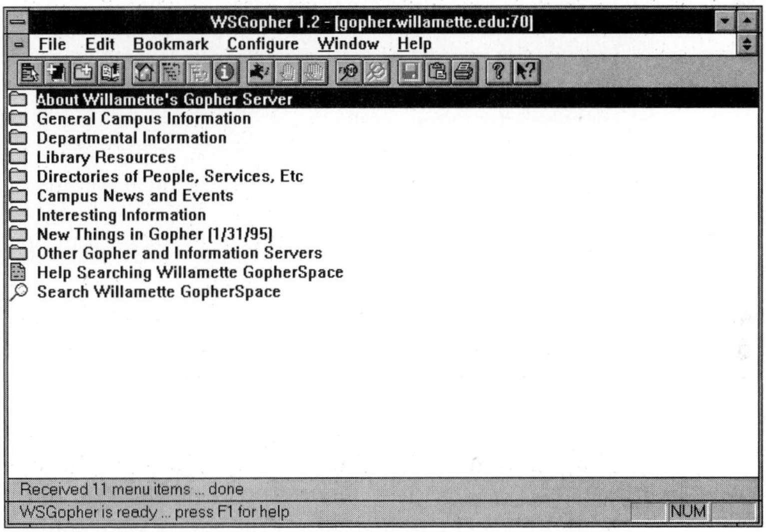

```
─────────────────────────────────────────────────────────────────
            WSGopher 1.2 - [gopher.willamette.edu:70]         ▼ ▲
─  File  Edit  Bookmark  Configure  Window  Help              ▲▼
 [toolbar icons]
 🗀 About Willamette's Gopher Server
 🗀 General Campus Information
 🗀 Departmental Information
 🗀 Library Resources
 🗀 Directories of People, Services, Etc
 🗀 Campus News and Events
 🗀 Interesting Information
 🗀 New Things in Gopher (1/31/95)
 🗀 Other Gopher and Information Servers
 📄 Help Searching Willamette GopherSpace
 🔍 Search Willamette GopherSpace




 Received 11 menu items ... done
 WSGopher is ready ... press F1 for help                    NUM
─────────────────────────────────────────────────────────────────
```

FIGURE 5.7

```
─────────────────────────────────────────────────────────────
                  Fetch this Gopher Item
       Title: [_____]    [ Paste  ]
 Server name: [_____]
 Server port: [70    ]                               [  OK    ]
    Selector: [_____]
   Item type: [Directory      ▼]  ☐ Gopher+  ☐ Ask form  [ Cancel ]
         URL: [_____]    [ Help   ]
─────────────────────────────────────────────────────────────
```

In the Server Name field, type **liberty.uc.wlu.edu** and click OK or press (ENTER).

The Gopher menu from Washington and Lee University, similar to the one shown in Figure 5.8, is displayed.

Select Explore Internet Resources by double-clicking on it.

The Explore Internet Resources menu is displayed, similar to the one shown in Figure 5.9.

Select Telnet Login to Sites (Hytelnet) by double-clicking on it.

The Telnet Login to Sites (Hytelnet) menu is displayed, similar to the one shown in Figure 5.10.

You are now using the Hytelnet program using Gopher. Take a minute to read the screen to see what types of information are available. Since we have already looked at a library catalog, let's select Other Resources.

Select Other Resources by double-clicking on it.

A screen, similar to Figure 5.11, is displayed.

FIGURE 5.8

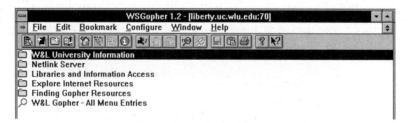

FIGURE 5.9

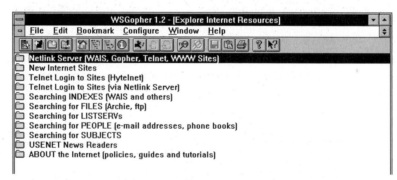

FIGURE 5.10

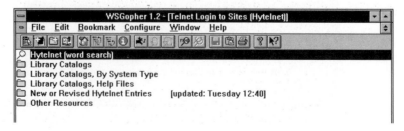

As you can see, many types of resources are available via Telnet, including resources listed in other chapters of this book. As we are interested in literature, English literature in particular, let's choose the Databases and bibliographies option.

Select Databases and bibliographies by double-clicking on it.

A screen similar to Figure 5.12 is displayed.

Notice that this screen contains diverse items, covering diverse topics. Take a moment to scroll through the screen.

In our quest for journal literature on Toni Morrison, let's take a look at CARL System Database Gateway.

Select CARL System Database Gateway by double-clicking on it.

You should see a menu similar to the one shown in Figure 5.13.

FIGURE 5.11

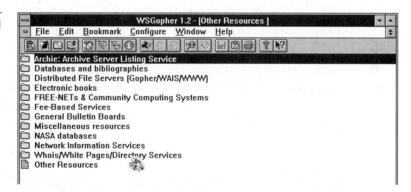

FIGURE 5.12

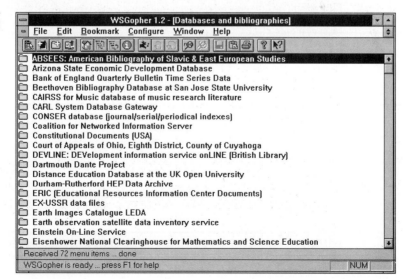

FIGURE 5.13

Notice that in Figure 5.13, the same option is listed twice but with a different icon in front of each. The icon tells you the type of option; the second selection, with a document icon in front, is, of course, a document.

 Select the second option with the document icon in front.

Information on the CARL System Database Gateway is displayed, as shown in Figure 5.14.

The document tells you that you can access CARL by Telnetting to database.carl.org or 192.54.81.76 and selecting vt100 as the terminal type. Be sure to note this information.

 Go back one screen so that the one similar to Figure 5.13 is displayed.

The first option, with an icon of a computer, will let you start an actual Telnet session to the CARL Database. You may want to try this option on your own. For now, however, you will exit Gopher and Telnet to CARL yourself.

 From the File menu, select Exit.

You've exited the Gopher program.

FIGURE 5.14

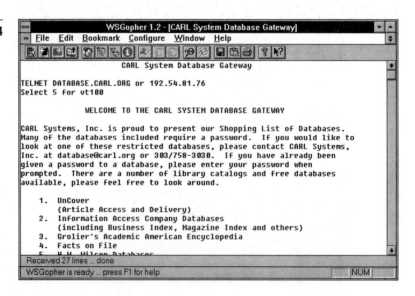

Telnet to database.carl.org and select 5. VT100 as the terminal type. Make sure to press (ENTER) after each command. Remember, you are no longer in the Windows environment. Hence, you have to select and press (ENTER).

You should see a screen similar to Figure 5.15.

This is the opening screen for the system at CARL (The Colorado Alliance of Research Libraries). The message onscreen describes the restrictions and cost involved in using this service. It also tells you that if you want to leave at any time, type **//EXIT**. You want to use the UnCover option, an open (free) access journal article index with full text delivery options (for a fee).

 Type **1** and press (ENTER).

For the next three screens, you are informed of the access options for Un-Cover. You just want to browse through for now, so you can ignore these.

 Press (ENTER) several times, until you reach an UnCover welcome message similar to the one shown in Figure 5.16.

Like many remote systems, it is hard to guess how to search them without reading the help screens. You can take a moment to read them, or just give it a shot. Here, you are going to do a Word search, since you want articles *about* Toni Morrison. (If you use Author search here, you will retrieve articles *by* Toni Morrison, and that is not what you want.)

FIGURE 5.15

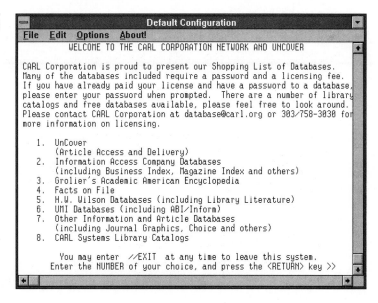

FIGURE 5.16

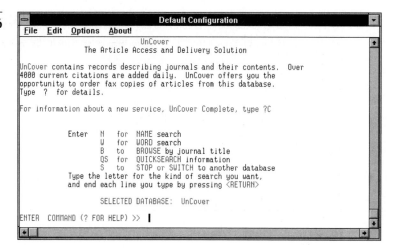

Type **W** and press (ENTER).

A screen similar to Figure 5.17 is displayed.

Again, the instructions onscreen tell you how to enter words for searching.

Type **Toni Morrison** and press (ENTER).

A screen similar to Figure 5.18 is displayed.

You should now see the number of citations retrieved. You are also asked whether you wish to enter a new word or display what you've retrieved. You will display the list of titles.

FIGURE 5.17

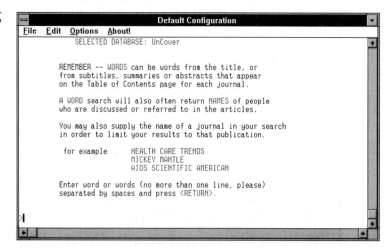

FIGURE 5.18

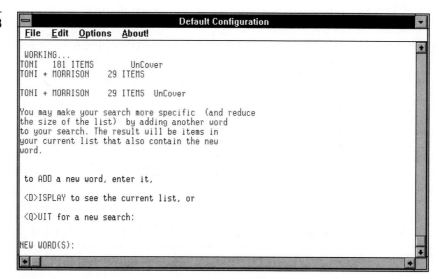

```
                           Default Configuration
 File   Edit   Options   About!

 WORKING...
TONI    181 ITEMS        UnCover
TONI + MORRISON     29 ITEMS

TONI + MORRISON     29 ITEMS  UnCover

You may make your search more specific  (and reduce
the size of the list)  by adding another word
to your search. The result will be items in
your current list that also contain the new
word.


 to ADD a new word, enter it,

 <D>ISPLAY to see the current list, or

 <Q>UIT for a new search:


NEW WORD(S):
```

Type D and press (ENTER).

A list of articles, similar to the one shown in Figure 5.19, is displayed.

You should now see a list of titles of journal articles and the names and dates of the journals in which the articles appeared. You can see the rest of the list by pressing (ENTER).

Press (ENTER).

FIGURE 5.19

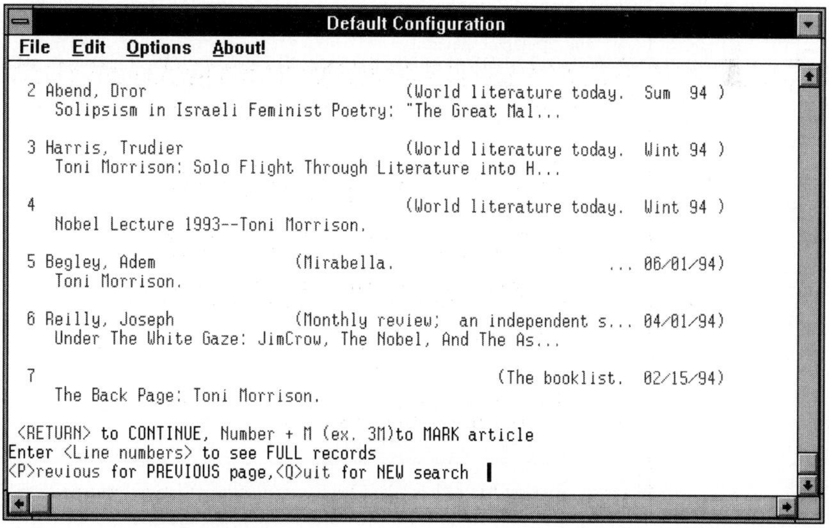

```
                           Default Configuration
 File   Edit   Options   About!

 2 Abend, Dror                     (World literature today.  Sum  94 )
    Solipsism in Israeli Feminist Poetry: "The Great Mal...

 3 Harris, Trudier                 (World literature today.  Wint 94 )
    Toni Morrison: Solo Flight Through Literature into H...

 4                                 (World literature today.  Wint 94 )
    Nobel Lecture 1993--Toni Morrison.

 5 Begley, Adem            (Mirabella.               ... 06/01/94)
    Toni Morrison.

 6 Reilly, Joseph          (Monthly review; an independent s... 04/01/94)
    Under The White Gaze: JimCrow, The Nobel, And The As...

 7                                 (The booklist.  02/15/94)
    The Back Page: Toni Morrison.

 <RETURN> to CONTINUE, Number + M (ex. 3M)to MARK article
Enter <Line numbers> to see FULL records
<P>revious for PREVIOUS page,<Q>uit for NEW search |
```

Notice that the articles are listed in reverse chronological order. You may want to take note of when articles began appearing in this database. Often, online information does not cover older material. You may want to check print indexes for older resources. Selecting a line number will display the full citation of an article. Select an article that looks interesting to you, say, 1.

Type 1 and press (ENTER).

More detailed information is shown, as displayed in Figure 5.20.

This gives you the information you need to get the article from your library, or if you'd rather purchase the article from CARL, that information is also given. These articles can help you in writing your paper on Toni Morrison. This article will give you a bibliography extending back to 1975, which may be useful!

NOTE: Oftentimes, when you are searching databases, it is useful to save the information that appears in the session window. Telnet can be set to capture the session to a file, so that everything transmitted and received is written to a file along with being displayed to the screen. To turn on the Capture feature, open the File menu and select Log Session to File.

It's time to leave this database. As you recall, the instructions onscreen told you to type **//EXIT** to leave the system. Why don't you try doing this part on your own!

Exit the database and then quit the Telnet program.

FIGURE 5.20

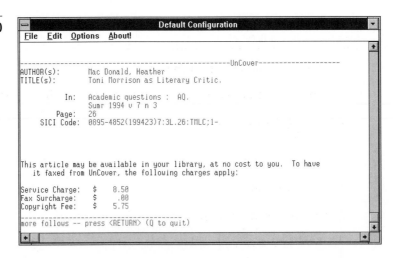

SUMMARY

In this chapter, many of the terms and concepts necessary to use Telnet are introduced:

+ Telnet allows you to connect directly to another computer system.

+ When you Telnet to another system, you have to learn the commands for that computer system. Some systems require that you have an account on their system.

+ You must know either the domain name or the IP address of the computer system to which you wish to connect.

+ If you get stuck in another computer, quit from the Telnet program by pulling down the File menu and selecting Exit.

+ Some systems will require that you specify the terminal type. Most likely, you are using vt100.

+ The Hytelnet database is a compilation of many useful Telnet addresses.

KEY TERMS

domain name	IP address	terminal emulation
Hytelnet	Telnet	

REVIEW QUESTIONS

1. What does Telnet allow you to do?

2. Do you need an account on the computer to which you connect?

3. If you get stuck while connected to another computer system, what can you do?

4. What is the difference between a domain name and an IP address?

5. What is Hytelnet?

6. Give two methods of accessing the Hytelnet database.

7. What terminal type is the most common when using Telnet?

EXERCISES

1. Using Hytelnet, find the library nearest you whose catalog is accessible via the Internet. Connect to that catalog and determine what books there are on the subject of United States history.

2. Suppose you are reading William Faulkner's *The Sound and the Fury* in your English class, and you are wondering if William Faulkner has written any other books, or if anyone has written books about him. How could you answer this question using Telnet? Can you find three books by or about William Faulkner?

3. Telnet to database.carl.org. This service offers many databases, some of which are fee-based, and some of which are free. You should be able to get to the main menu just by pressing (ENTER) in response to the numerous questions asked. Locate the menu option Carl Uncover. Use this database to determine whether any recent magazine articles have been published about mental illness among the homeless. *Hint:* Use the W word search function!

4. Telnet to sjsulib1.sjsu.edu or 130.65.100.1. From the menu displayed, select D on the main menu, then Beethoven Bibliography Database. Search this database to identify works that deal with Beethoven's deafness. Also, see if you can find any works that compare Beethoven to Schumann.

5. Telnet to the Library of Congress Information System, locis.loc.gov, to determine whether there has been any recent legislation regarding the National Information Infostructure. *Hint:* You will not find this in the Library of Congress Catalog!

DISCUSSION TOPICS

1. What are some of the difficulties you may run into using Telnet?

2. Assuming that you've already used other Internet tools, discuss the merits of Telnet compared to other tools.

WS_FTP AND ARCHIE (FTP)
Getting It From There to Here (and Back Again)

CHAPTER **6**

OBJECTIVES

Upon completing the material presented in this chapter, you should understand the following aspects of the Internet:

✦ The concept behind File Transfer Protocol (FTP)
✦ How to perform an FTP session using WS_FTP
✦ How to move among directories
✦ How to locate files
✦ How to transfer files
✦ How to identify file types
✦ How to use Archie to find files

BEFORE YOU START

In order to perform online exercises in this chapter, you need the following:

✦ An IBM PC compatible running Windows and connected to the Internet
✦ Installed copies of the WS_FTP and Telnet software on the machine you are using. Software used here are WS_FTP version 95.04.24 and Uwterm, version 0.97i.

WHAT IS THE FILE TRANSFER PROTOCOL?

As by now you're aware, the Internet is like a vast ocean—people and information as far as the eye can see (or, rather, the fingers can type). Telnet can take you to other places, there are tools to find information, there are tools to help you navigate around—but sometimes you simply want to get a file from over there and bring it over here.

The **File Transfer Protocol (FTP)** provides a way for files to be transferred between computers on the Internet. It permits you to connect to another computer on the Internet, then either put files on the other computer, or, as FTP is more commonly used, get files from the other computer back to your own local computer.

What sorts of files can you get with FTP? Almost any sort of file you can imagine. To name a few, you can find things like computer programs (for almost any kind of machine, including IBM PCs and compatibles), electronic texts, archives of mailing lists, and graphic images. Even if there were no other services available on the Internet, the files available from FTP are so numerous that one could spend a good portion of one's days simply sifting through archive after archive. The only catch is that in order to use FTP to retrieve a file, you have to know the name and the location of the file you want.

HOW DOES FTP WORK?

FTP uses the client/server model as do many other Internet tools. Through the use of client software, you can connect to remote FTP servers and request that files be sent from them. FTP will take care of all the nitty-gritty details—like moving the file across the network and dealing with different kinds of computers and operating systems on the Internet. So, even though one machine might be using UNIX and another might be using Windows, it makes no difference while you're using FTP to transfer the document. The retrieved document is placed on the machine that has the client software running. That means if you use Windows computer that runs FTP, the retrieved file is placed on your Windows computer.

BOX 6.1 | **USING FTP TO OBTAIN SOFTWARE**

One thing that you'll often use FTP for is to obtain software over the Internet. The ways in which you obtain software are the same as the methods described to transfer files in this chapter. However, there are a few additional steps involved. *Continued on next page*

BOX 6.1

USING FTP TO OBTAIN SOFTWARE (*continued*)

The first thing to be aware of is that the files that you find are either binary or text (ASCII). A software file is binary, and you need to make certain that it is being retrieved as such. In WS_FTP, you need to specify the format by clicking on the appropriate radio button.

Once you've retrieved software, you may find that it is compressed. Software is often **compressed** to save space during transfer, but you must then decompress it in order for it to be useful. To decompress it, you will need compression software. Listed below are the file extensions that indicate what kind of compression has been used on a file, as well as what software package you can use to decompress that file. Be aware that more than one kind of compression can be used on a file, which can result in several extensions, such as .sit.hqx. As you might have guessed, decompression software packages are also available via FTP!

Extension	Package
.z	Unpack, on most UNIX machines
.Z	Uncompress, on most UNIX machines
.gz	Gunzip, on some UNIX machines
.sit	UnStuffit, for Macintoshes
.hqx	UnStuffit, for Macintoshes
.zip	PkUnzip, for IBM PCs
.zoo	Zoo, for IBM PCs
.arc	Arc, PkArc, or PkPak, for IBM PCs
.arj	Arj, for IBM PCs
.lzh	Lha, for IBM PCs

You will need to obtain a copy of PkUnzip in order to decompress most software for Windows or MS-DOS that you will find. PkUnzip is also available via anonymous FTP, at the host wuarchive.wustl.edu in the directory /systems/ibmpc/umich/edu/compressions/zip, as the file pkz204g.

There are some large archives of software available for you to explore. Try:

wuarchive.wustl.edu	A huge software repository for many different computers, including MS-DOS and Windows
oak.oakland.edu	This archive site has a mirror of the SimTel archives, a large archive of MS-DOS programs. The original SimTel is no longer online, so the only way the files can be accessed is through this and other mirrors.

NOTE: If you transfer a UNIX or Macintosh computer program to your Windows machine, you may not be able to use it.

How does FTP differ from something like Gopher? The biggest difference is that FTP servers aren't connected to each other in the way that Gopher servers are. In GopherSpace, you can wander around from server to server and never realize when you've left the one and begun to browse the other. You can get anywhere just by following the menus. With FTP, you have to connect to each server. Once you've connected to a server, you can browse through the available files. If you want to retrieve files available on another server, you'll have to explicitly connect to that server yourself.

NOTE: You will find that many of the names of FTP servers start with the acronym ftp, such as ftp.nevada.edu and ftp.uu.net.

In this chapter, you will use WS_FTP, an FTP client program for Windows. In order to use WS_FTP to transfer a file, you need to know the following: (1) how to start an FTP session, specifying the FTP server you want to access; (2) how to move through the directory structure on the FTP server to locate the document you seek; (3) how to retrieve the document; and (4) how to quit the FTP session.

In this exercise, you will learn how to find useful information with FTP, such as subject-oriented compilations of reference information, some political science information from the White House, and some online electronic texts.

GETTING ON AND OFF

Let's start with the basics: how to get into (and how to get back out of) FTP. As mentioned earlier, you need to know the address of the FTP site you want to access. The site you'll use is pit-manager.mit.edu, a wonderful archive of the Usenet Frequently Asked Questions (FAQs) lists. Briefly, a FAQ is a compilation of those questions frequently asked on certain topics. The sci.space FAQ, for instance, is a huge compilation of useful (volunteer-contributed) answers to astronomical and spaceflight-related questions. Although Usenet and FAQs were discussed in Chapter 3, they are such wonderful resources that it makes perfect sense to begin the discussion of FTP here.

 Visually locate the WS_FTP program icon in the Program Manager window. It should look similar to the one shown below.

WS_FTP

To start WS_FTP, double-click on the WS_FTP icon.

A dialog box similar to the one shown in Figure 6.1 appears.

You must specify Host <u>N</u>ame, <u>U</u>ser ID, and Password. There are also some additional fields (including Host Type, Account, Remote Host, and Local PC), but you may leave those alone. Some of the boxes may already contain entries. You can change these the same way you change an entry in any Windows application.

WS_FTP provides preconfigured "session profiles." Each session profile contains information about a particular host which you access often with FTP. If you click on the down arrow key to the right of the Profile Name: field, a pull-down menu appears listing FTP sites which have been predefined (most of which are archives of Windows software). If you were to select any of these options, the Host Name and other necessary fields would be automatically filled out.

Right now, you will connect to pit-manager.mit.edu—a site that is not defined. You can specify a new connection by clicking on the Ne<u>w</u> button in the Session Profile dialog box.

NOTE: As with any Windows application, you can select a button by holding down the (ALT) key and pressing the underlined character in the command name. For example, you can select the Ne<u>w</u> button by holding down the (ALT) key and pressing **W**.

Click the Ne<u>w</u> button.

All of the fields go blank, except the Host Type field.

In the Host Name field, enter **pit-manager.mit.edu.**

NOTE: To position the cursor in a field, you can either click in the field's text box with the mouse or press the (TAB) key.

FIGURE 6.1

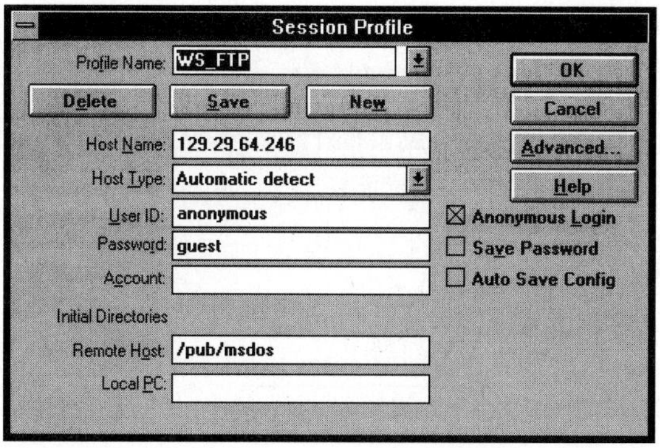

Session Profile

Pro<u>f</u>ile Name: WS_FTP ▼	OK
<u>D</u>elete <u>S</u>ave Ne<u>w</u>	Cancel
Host <u>N</u>ame: 129.29.64.246	<u>A</u>dvanced...
Host <u>T</u>ype: Automatic detect ▼	Help
<u>U</u>ser ID: anonymous	☒ Anonymous <u>L</u>ogin
<u>P</u>assword: guest	☐ Sa<u>v</u>e Password
A<u>c</u>count:	☐ Auto Save Config
Initial Directories	
Remote Host: /pub/msdos	
Local <u>P</u>C:	

BOX 6.2

FULL-PRIVILEGE FTP

FTP has two access modes. The first is *anonymous* FTP. The second, which you'll probably use less often, is called *full-privilege* FTP. In this latter style of FTP, you'll actually login to a computer on which you have an account, much as you'd log into a UNIX-based machine (if you have an account on one).

If you have an account on a machine running an FTP server (that is, if you have a username and password that allow you to login), it is likely that you can take advantage of full-privilege FTP. If not, skip the rest of this box.

To see whether you can use this type of FTP, try opening a connection to the machine on which you have an account. When asked for your username, provide the one with which you normally login (for instance, jsmith). When asked for a password, provide your normal password. If your password is accepted, then you have full FTP privileges!

What does this get you? For one, you can retrieve the files that you've stored on that machine, and you can also store other files there. This kind of FTP access is most useful if you want to get files off of that computer onto the computer which you are currently at, which may be thousands of miles away!

You can use full-privilege FTP just as you use anonymous FTP.

There are two ways to connect to an FTP site: full-privilege and anonymous. You are using **anonymous FTP** when you type **anonymous** as the User ID and your e-mail address as the password. Anonymous FTP is a common service on FTP servers. Although FTP was originally designed to provide access to only the legitimate users of the machine (what is now called **full-privilege FTP**), when a need to come up with a scheme to make files available to the general public arose, anonymous FTP was devised. When you find a reference to information available via FTP, you can be sure (unless specifically told otherwise) that it's available using anonymous FTP.

 In the User ID field, enter **anonymous**.

Enter your e-mail address in the Password: field. (If you do not have an e-mail address, use **guest** as your password.)

The dialog box should look similar to the one shown in Figure 6.2.

NOTE: You can also check the Anonymous Login checkbox in the Session Profile dialog box. This will automatically fill in the User ID: and Password: fields with anonymous and guest, respectively.

FIGURE 6.2

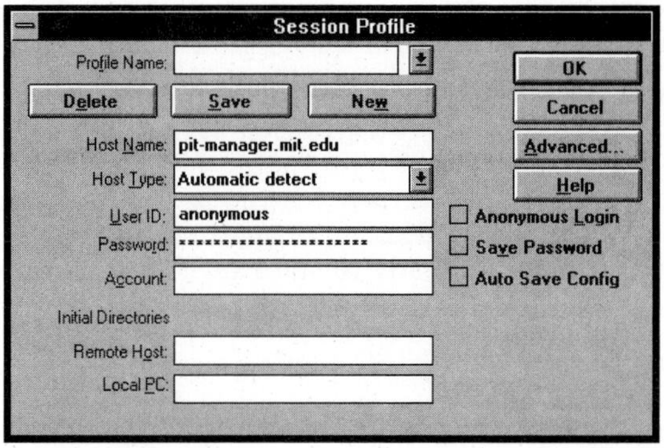

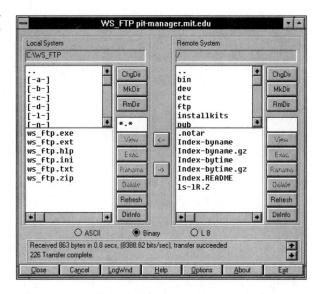

If you know exactly where to locate the file you seek, you can specify the directory, or the location, in the Remote Host: field. However, since you can browse through the FTP server to find the file, there is no need to make an entry in this field.

NOTE: If you want to save this session profile so that it will appear on the pull-down menu, specify a session name in the Profile Name field and click on the Save button.

 Click OK or press (ENTER) to connect to pit-manager.mit.edu.

After taking a moment to connect, a screen similar to the one shown in Figure 6.3 is displayed.

FIGURE 6.3

NOTE: If the FTP site is unavailable or not a known host, WS_FTP will inform you of this. All status messages are displayed in an area near the bottom of the window, right above the Cancel, Help, and Exit buttons. You can try the connection again using the Connect button at the bottom of the window. This will bring up the Session Profile dialog box.

At this point, you are ready to start an FTP session with this server. Right now, however, you will simply quit the session.

 Click on the Close button.

The connection is closed, and WS_FTP is ready to open a connection to another server.

If you want to quit WS_FTP entirely, click on the Exit button.

FTP DIRECTORY STRUCTURE

Once you're inside an FTP server, you'll want to get yourself oriented. FTP servers organize files in what's known as a **hierarchical file structure**. It is a tree-like structure—there is a root directory with a number of subdivisions, or subdirectories, each containing files and other subdirectories with a common subject matter.

Figure 6.4 is a rough presentation of the FTP directories at pit-manager. mit.edu. Brackets denote a directory. It is an upside-down tree structure. The top is the root of the directory. At the root level are files like Index-byname and directories like [bin], [dev], and [pub]. Most often, the pub directory contains files available to anonymous FTP users.

Within the pub directory, you find some files like WorldMap and directories like [usenet-by-group]. Moving right along, within the Usenet directory is a directory called [sci.space.science], and finally, within that, you find FAQ documents on space science.

The location of the file is listed by giving the directory levels separated by a forward slash (/). For example, to specify the location of file Space-FAQ as shown in Figure 6.4, someone would say that the file is found at /pub/usenet-by-group/sci.space.science/. Knowing this, you can then navigate through those directories or specify it in the Directory field in the Open Connection dialog box.

MOVING ABOUT IN THE FTP DIRECTORY STRUCTURE

Now, this is all fine when you've got a road map, like the diagram in the last section, or the specific location of the file you seek. Instead, you'll most likely find

FIGURE 6.4

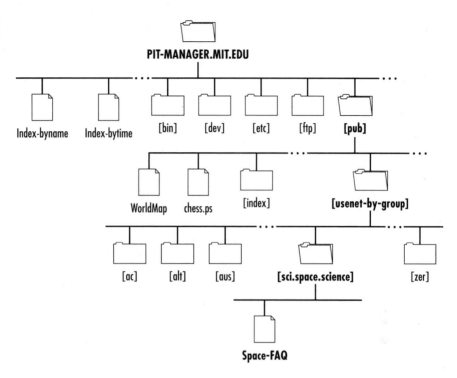

yourself taking a look around to find out what directories and files exist for you to explore. You can then move from directory to directory, one step at a time.

 Reconnect to pit-manager.mit.edu using anonymous FTP. If you have not quit WS_FTP, then you can simply click on the Connect button to display the Session Profile dialog box.

After a moment, you will be reconnected to pit-manager.mit.edu and the screen displays a window similar to the one in Figure 6.5.

The main window for WS_FTP is divided into four parts, as labeled in Figure 6.5. On the left is information about files and directories on *your* computer. The current directory shown is where downloaded files will be placed. On the right is information about files and directories on the remote computer being accessed (in this case, pit-manager). Furthermore, the local and remote sections are broken down even further: The top half is information about subdirectories, and the bottom half is information about files which you can retrieve.

For example, in Figure 6.5, bin, dev, and etc are subdirectories on the remote system, whereas Index-bytime and Index.README are documents. Directories can be opened to examine contents and document files can be retrieved.

FIGURE 6.5

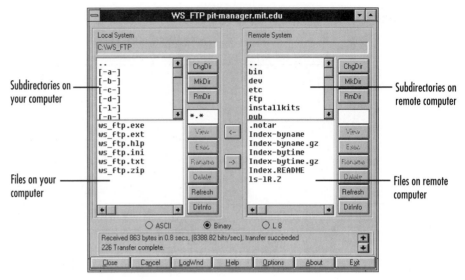

Subdirectories on your computer

Files on your computer

Subdirectories on remote computer

Files on remote computer

NOTE: WS_FTP does not automatically display information about the size of files, nor when they were created. If you would like to get this information, click on the Options button and then click on the Program Options button. Check the Show Full Directory Information checkbox. Size information is useful for estimating how long a file will take to retrieve. 300Kb makes a document roughly equal to the length of a novel, so some of these files are sizable. The larger the file, the longer it will take you to retrieve. The date at which the file was created is also important information for judging whether the document or program you want to receive might be too old (or too new) to be of any use.

To open a directory, double-click on it. To move back up a subdirectory level, select .. (two periods) in the Directories list. As with any other Windows application, if there are more directories or files than can display onscreen, vertical scroll bars appear.

Double-click on the directory pub to open it.

After a moment, you will get a listing of files in the directory pub as displayed in Figure 6.6.

As an anonymous FTP user, the pub directory is where you are most likely to find files to which you have access. As you scroll through the Directories list, you might notice a directory titled usenet-by-group. Since you are looking for Usenet FAQs, this is a very reasonable place to start.

Use the scroll bar in the Directories list to find usenet-by-group and double-click on it.

After a few moments (this is a large list, so be patient), you will see a list of files in this directory. Notice that the Files list is blank—there are no documents in this directory, only more subdirectories.

FIGURE 6.6

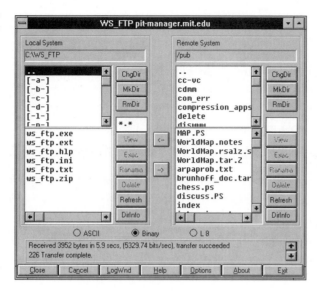

What you are seeing is a list of all newsgroups for which a FAQ exists. Each newsgroup has its own subdirectory, which contains the FAQs for that newsgroup. The huge number of newsgroups accounts for the huge number of subdirectories.

Let's say you're doing research for a paper on the development of space exploration. One place to check might be in the FAQ for sci.space.science, a Usenet newsgroup about space issues.

 Locate the subdirectory sci.space.science and double-click on it.

NOTE: If the filename is too long, WS_FTP does not show the entire name of the file in the window. To see the rest of the filenames, use the horizontal scroll bar on the listing window.

One that looks promising is Space_FAQ_08_13_-_Planetary_Probe_History.

Once you locate a file, you can copy it to your local computer. Remember, the left side of the window displays the information about the local computer. You need to specify the drive and directory on the local computer where you'd like the file copied. Letters enclosed in brackets indicate drives. For example, [-a-] means the A drive. Another thing you need to indicate is the type of file, which is discussed in more detail in Box 6.3. But for now, just select ASCII.

 Specify the drive and the directory on the local computer to which you want the file copied. Click to select ASCII.

You can retrieve a file in one of two ways:

✦ Select it by clicking on it once to highlight, then click on the <- button in the middle of your screen. (The left arrow moves files from the right side of your window—the remote computer—to the left side of your window—your local computer. The button with the right-pointing arrow does the opposite.)

✦ Double-click on the filename.

 Double-click on Space_FAQ_08_13_-_Planetary_Probe_History.

After a few moments, you will see a Transfer Status dialog box, which appears similar to the one shown in Figure 6.7. When the progress bar reaches 100%, the transfer will be complete.

What you've just done is to transfer a file that was on another computer onto your local computer. Unlike Gopher, you're not grabbing it and immediately displaying it. Instead, you've copied this file to your local computer. You can now do things with it, such as run it (if it is a program), or use it in a word processing application (if it is a document file).

 Close the connection.

EXAMINING THE DOCUMENT DURING FTP

Now let's try another example. Here's the situation.

It's the night before that paper on the North American Free Trade Agreement is due, and the government document archives offices are closed until morning. What you could really use are some primary sources, like the text of NAFTA itself. Fortunately for you, the White House is (partially) online!

The FTP server for the White House is ftp.whitehouse.gov.

 Start a new session to connect to ftp.whitehouse.gov as an anonymous user.

After a moment, you will be connected.

FIGURE 6.7

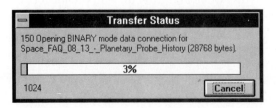

Notice again the pub directory.

Double-click on pub, then on political-science.

When you take a look at this directory, notice that one of the subdirectories is nafta.

Double-click on nafta.

There are two directories: full-text and nafta-notes. Because you are looking for the full text, you'll probably want to look in that directory.

Double-click on full-text.

It would be awfully nice if you could take a look at the contents of these many files without going through the process of retrieving a file and then later viewing it. It would be useful to be able to actually preview a document before transferring it to your own computer, making sure you are actually getting what you want.

Fortunately for you, you can do just that. The View button provides this functionality. Let's use it to take a look at chap-01.txt.

Select chap-01.txt by clicking on it.

Click the View button on the right side of the WS_FTP window.

The file is displayed in a new window (using the Notepad program supplied with Windows), similar to that shown in Figure 6.8.

FIGURE 6.8

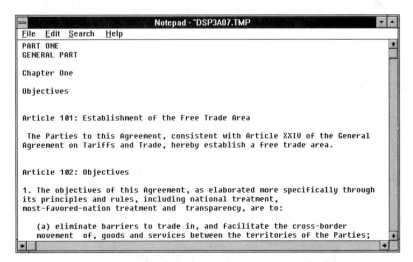

NOTE: The size of the file that Notepad can display is limited. It is possible to choose an alternate text viewer. This is done by clicking the Options button on the main screen, clicking the Program Options button, then entering the full pathname of the alternate program in the Text Viewer box.

 When you're done reading the file, close the window by opening the File menu and selecting Exit.

Should you decide that this is the document you need, you can retrieve it as was done before.

There you go! These basic functions—getting in, taking a look around, moving to where the file is, and getting back out again—are the better part of what you need to know to use FTP effectively. In fact, there's really only one other thing you need to know how to do, and that's how to find the files you want to retrieve.

 Close the connection.

Make sure to exit WS_FTP by clicking the Exit button.

ARCHIE: USER-INDEX OF ANONYMOUS FTP

FTP—in fact, the entire Internet—can certainly be overwhelming. A huge number of FTP sites is available, and it's not always clear what piece of information is where. But don't despair! There is a silver lining to this cloud, a lining named **Archie**.

Archie was the first of the so-called "resource discovery tools" of the Internet (other tools, such as Veronica and the W3 Catalog, are described in other chapters). Archie's name is an abbreviation of the word "archives." While it wasn't named after the comic book character, it has spawned a few imitators, the most infamous being Veronica, which provides a similar service for Gopher.

BOX 6.3 | ## DECIPHERING THE WS_FTP DIALOG BOX

The more adventurous among you may be wondering what some of the information in your WS_FTP window actually *means*. It can be a little bit overwhelming at first, so here's a quick guide to what's what.

The window is divided into two halves. The left half represents files found on your own computer—the *local system.* The right half represents files found on the computer you are using FTP to get files from—the *remote system.*

Continued on next page

BOX 6.3

DECIPHERING THE WS_FTP DIALOG BOX (*continued*)

Each half is subdivided into two quarters. The top quarter is a list of all of the subdirectories of the directory you are currently in. You can use this quarter to navigate around in either the local or remote system's file structure. (Remember that ".." means "go back to the directory just above the current one.") The bottom quarter is a list of all of the current directory's files. These are the files you can retrieve or view using FTP.

Between the left and right halves are two buttons. One button points left, and one button points right. The button pointing left moves files "to the left"—that is, it moves them from the remote system (on the right side of your screen) to the local system (on the left). This is the button you'd use to retrieve files. The button pointing right does the opposite; it moves files from the local system to the remote system. You can do this only when you are using full-privilege FTP (see Box 6.2).

Each half also has a set of buttons associated with it, such as ChgDir, View, and Rename. The buttons on the left will affect files or directories on the local system—so the left View button will let you view a file on your own machine. The buttons on the right will affect files on the remote system—so the right ChgDir button will let you change to a new directory on the remote system. Don't get confused about which set of buttons affects which system!

The radio buttons ASCII, Binary, and L8 allow you to specify what kind of file you are retrieving. If you are retrieving a text file (one rule of thumb is that a text file is any file meant to be read by humans, not computers), you should select the ASCII setting. However, if you are downloading a program for your computer to run, you should select Binary. L8 is a special setting for the VMS operating system. We won't cover it here (and you probably don't need to worry about it). Just remember, if you grab a file via FTP and you don't get what you expected, switch from ASCII to Binary mode (or vice versa) and try again.

Below the radio buttons is a short status line screen. This displays information about your FTP connection. Most of the messages displayed are FTP messages intended for computers, so don't worry about it if they don't make too much sense. If you want help interpreting these messages, ask your teacher or technical support staff.

Finally, at the bottom, there are several buttons which affect your overall FTP session. The <u>C</u>lose (or <u>C</u>onnect—this button changes depending on whether you are actually connected to an FTP server or not) button will either close your current FTP session or open a new one. The E<u>x</u>it button will exit WS_FTP. And, most importantly, the <u>H</u>elp button will bring up online help which can help you to learn about the features we lack space to cover here.

What Archie provides is roughly analogous to the card catalogs of libraries past. Specifically, it provides something very similar to a catalog of the *titles* of books in a library. You can then search this catalog and find files on the Internet by their titles.

Archie accomplishes this feat by keeping track of nearly all of the anonymous FTP sites. Once a month, it searches these sites, compiling a list of all files. Then, once it has compiled its database, it sits content, waiting for queries from users.

As you may suspect and expect, Archie is also based upon clients and servers. In this case, it is the server that searches FTP sites and maintains a huge database, and it is the client that asks the server to yield up this information to the user.

Armed with this quick introduction to Archie, let's jump into learning by example, and demonstrate what Archie does. At the same time, you will see the wealth of electronically available texts on the Internet.

USING ARCHIE

Here is the situation:

You're doing an analysis of *A Midsummer Night's Dream* for a literature class. It occurs to you that there are some interesting contrasts to be drawn between the way Shakespeare depicts love in this play, as opposed to how he approaches it in another of his well-known pieces, *Romeo and Juliet.* Playing off of these contrasts would give you a nice conclusion to the piece, providing an opportunity to tie it all into Elizabethan attitudes towards love.

It's just too bad that the nearest copy of *Romeo and Juliet* is over at the library, and you're in the computer center trying to work on your paper (and zealously guarding your computer from the few people who are standing at the door, enviously eyeing your seat). However, you've heard that the Internet has some electronic texts online, so why not check whether it has *Romeo and Juliet?*

To check whether *Romeo and Juliet* is available via FTP, you need to use Archie. You will use the Archie at archie.sura.net by Telnetting to the site. If you are not familiar with Telnet, just follow the instructions given here. (Telnet is described in Chapter 5.)

NOTE: Although an Archie client exists for Windows, it was not very reliable at the time of this writing. Ask your instructor about the availability of an updated version.

Visually locate the Telnet (Uwterm, in this case) icon in the Program Manager window. It should look similar to the one below.

Uwterm

Double-click on the Telnet (Uwterm) icon to start a Telnet session.

The Telnet to dialog box should appear. If not, open the Options menu, then select Host/Port. The Telnet to dialog box appears.

In the Host Name field, enter archie.sura.net.

Click on OK or press (ENTER).

After a moment, you will be connected to the host archie.sura.net and a session window, as shown in Figure 6.9, is displayed.

Type qarchie and press (ENTER).

Some introductory text will appear, followed by a prompt (archie>) indicating that Archie is ready to accept commands. The screen will be similar to the one shown in Figure 6.10.

One of the main commands used in qarchie is prog *<filename>*. Use it to execute a search for *<filename>* using the current search type.

FIGURE 6.9

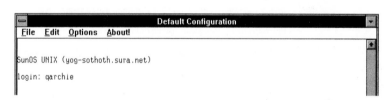

```
┌─────────────────── Default Configuration ───────────────────┐
│ File   Edit   Options   About!                               │
├──────────────────────────────────────────────────────────────┤
│ SunOS UNIX (yog-sothoth.sura.net)                            │
│                                                               │
│ login: qarchie                                               │
└──────────────────────────────────────────────────────────────┘
```

FIGURE 6.10

```
┌─────────────────── Default Configuration ───────────────────┐
│ File   Edit   Options   About!                               │
├──────────────────────────────────────────────────────────────┤
│ Last login: Mon Feb 27 03:09:28 from pc_11B09.uc3m.es        │
│ SunOS Release 4.1.3 (NYARLATHOTEP) #3: Thu Apr 22 15:26:21 EDT 1993 │
│                                                               │
│                    Welcome to Archie!                        │
│                     Version 3.2.2                            │
│                                                               │
│ SURAnet is pleased to announce the release of archie with a new version of │
│ archie software.                                             │
│                                                               │
│ If you need help with the interactive client type 'help' at the 'archie>' │
│ prompt. If you have any questions, please read help >>FIRST<<, then if │
│ your question was not answered send e-mail to 'archie-admin@sura.net' │
│                                                               │
│ archie-admin.                                                │
│ (January 23,1995)                                            │
│                                                               │
│ # Bunyip Information Systems, 1993, 1994                     │
│                                                               │
│ # Terminal type set to 'vt100 24 80'.                        │
│ # 'erase' character is '^?'.                                 │
│ # 'search' (type string) has the value 'sub'.                │
│ archie>                                                      │
└──────────────────────────────────────────────────────────────┘
```

As *<filename>*, you enter the search string that might be used to locate the file. This is a search based on the filename. The problem is that the titles of files at FTP sites are often less than descriptive. For example, titles might range from "romeo.juliet.1.cpt.hqx" to "Romeo.And.Juliet.gz." So rather than entering "romeo.and.juliet," you will enter just the one word "juliet."

NOTE: Archie permits several different types of searches. The one that it uses by default is called "Case Insensitive Substring," meaning that "juliet" will match any title that contains the word "juliet" and might have "juliet" capitalized. So, we'd match things like: "juliet.fries," "RomeoAndJuliet," "this-name-has-juLiEt-in-it."

Remember that often, case matters. Uppercase and lowercase aren't always the same thing to computers, and "juliet" might be considered to be different from "Juliet."

You might use another type of search, such as an "exact" search, if you knew more precisely the filename you sought. So, if you knew there was a file called "romeo.and.juliet," and wanted to find only it, you might do an exact search on "romeo.and.juliet."

 Type prog juliet and press (ENTER).

Archie will search for all file titles containing the word "juliet." After a minute or two, a list will appear, similar to the one shown in Figure 6.11.

You can use the scroll bar to see the entire list. However, you may need some help in understanding the result you get back.

FIGURE 6.11

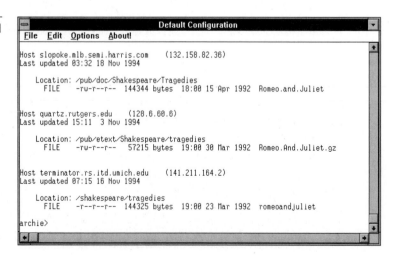

NOTE: These are the results obtained as this book was going to press. The results of your search may be dramatically different.

Let's look at some samples:

```
Host faui43.informatik.uni-erlangen.de    (131.188.31.3)
Last updated 07:18 17 Oct 1994


    Location: /mounts/epix/public/pub/Mac/system.extensions/font/type1
    FILE   -r--r--r--  39669 bytes  19:00 19 Sep 1992  juliet.cpt.hqx
```

The information about "host" is the name of the FTP site on which this file is available (for anonymous access, naturally). It is faui43.informatik.uni-erlangen.de, in this case, meaning that it is in Germany (*de* is the two-letter country code for Germany—at least on the Internet). The next piece of information is the location—the directories where the files are located. In this case you would look in the directory mounts, then epix, then public, then pub, then Mac, then system extensions, then font, and then in the directory type1 in order to find this file, named "juliet.cpt.hqx."

This time, notice that the extension has both .cpt and .hqx in the filename. Again, these are both compression formats—for the Apple Macintosh. If it weren't for the fact that this looked like a font, we'd be set.

```
Host sunsite.unc.edu


    Location: /pub/docs/books/shakespeare/tragedies
    FILE -rw-r--r--   63999  Aug 26 1992  romeoandjuliet.Z
```

The host is sunsite.unc.edu. To find the file you would go to pub, then docs, then books, then shakespeare, then tragedies. "romeoandjuliet.Z" is the file-name. The extension ".Z" also means a compressed format, but one used by UNIX computers. This sounds closer to what you want—the location includes the word Shakespeare, and the title has both "romeo" and "juliet" in it. However, since you're not on a UNIX machine, you're not quite home free yet.

```
Host monu6.cc.monash.edu.au
    Location:/pub/win3/fonts/atm
      FILE -rw-rw-r--29472   Oct 28 1992   Juliet.zip
```

The host is monu6.cc.monash.edu.au, an FTP site in Australia. To find the file you would go to pub, then to win3, then fonts, and finally into atm. Finally, there is a line of information much like the information displayed on the Directories list box. The final piece of information is the name of the file, "juliet.zip."

Some clues indicate that this is not what you want—most notably, the fact that the location includes the word "fonts." This is probably a font for Microsoft Windows, indicated by "win3," instead of what you seek.

Something else to be aware of is the .zip in the filename. ".zip" indicates that this is a compressed file. Compression is a software process that shrinks the size of a file, making it easier to store and faster to transfer. Usually, a .zip file is for use by a machine running MS-DOS or Windows. You should remember that extension, though, when you're looking for MS-DOS or Windows files that aren't just text files.

NOTE: You will find many compressed files on FTP. The reason is very simple: Compressed files don't require as much storage and are faster to transfer.

Host terminator.rs.itd.umich.edu   (141.211.164.2)
Last updated 03:48 15 Oct 1994

  Location: /shakespeare/tragedies
    FILE   -r--r--r-- 144325 bytes 21:00 23 Mar 1992 romeoandjuliet

This one looks perfect. It doesn't seem to be compressed (no extensions), and it appears to be a Shakespearean tragedy. Bingo! Time to get it.

Scroll through your result from Archie to see if the listing from terminator.rs.itd.umich.edu is displayed.

Once you have the archie> prompt, type **quit** and press (ENTER).

Archie will quit, and your Telnet window may disappear.

If your Telnet window does not disappear, then open the File menu and select Exit.

The Telnet application will quit.

RETRIEVING A FILE

You will now retrieve the file from terminator.rs.itd.umich.edu.

Start WS_FTP.

Connect to terminator.rs.itd.umich.edu as an anonymous user.

FIGURE 6.12

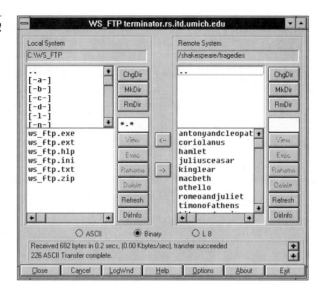

Now, locate the document.

Double-click on shakespeare in the Directories list.

Double-click on tragedies in the Directories list.

You will see a list of files, as shown in Figure 6.12.

As you might have expected, this archive contains more than just *Romeo and Juliet.* Serendipity can often play as important a role in discovering Internet resources as the effective use of tools such as Archie.

Close the connection and quit the FTP session.

And there you are—all the tools you need to successfully use FTP to find and retrieve files from across the Internet.

SUMMARY

In this chapter, many of the terms and concepts that are necessary to use FTP are introduced:

✦ The File Transfer Protocol (FTP) provides a way for files to be transferred between computers on the Internet.

✦ In order to use FTP, you must have access to FTP client software. The Windows client used here is WS_FTP.

✦ In order to use FTP, you must know the address of the FTP server you want to access.

✦ There are two types of FTP: anonymous FTP and full-privilege FTP. Anonymous FTP provides access to public files on the FTP server without an account on that computer. For full-privilege FTP, you need an account.

✦ The files on an FTP server are organized in a hierarchical file structure. You need to know how to move through the directory structure in order to access files.

✦ The files retrieved using FTP are stored on your own computer.

✦ Archie is an index of anonymous FTP files, categorized by titles.

✦ Many of the files stored at FTP sites are in compressed format. These files must be decompressed once retrieved.

KEY TERMS

anonymous FTP	compressed files	full-privilege FTP
Archie	File Transfer Protocol (FTP)	hierarchical file structure

REVIEW QUESTIONS

1. What is FTP?

2. What types of files can you transfer using FTP?

3. What is the difference between anonymous and full-privilege FTP?

4. When you retrieve a file using FTP, where does it get stored?

5. Explain how files are organized at an FTP site.

6. How do you move from one directory to another at an FTP site?

7. What FTP command do you give to actually transfer a file?

8. Can you look at a file you find at an FTP site before transferring it to your computer? How?

9. What is the purpose of Archie?

10. What does it mean to say that a file is compressed? What is the purpose of compressing a file?

EXERCISES

1. Find the FAQ for sci.physics.

2. Find the text of Edwin Abbott's *Flatland.*

3. How do you access the Smithsonian's collection of photographs? What categories of photographs do they have in their collection? How big is the collection? Specify how you discovered these things.

4. You heard about an organization called the Free Software Foundation. (They name their software after wildebeests . . . that's good gnus!) The organization keeps a large FTP site somewhere that contains all the software they produce for public consumption. Where is this FTP site, and what kinds of programs can you get there?

DISCUSSION TOPICS

1. What differences are there between using FTP to retrieve information on the Internet and using tools like Gopher and the World Wide Web? What kinds of similarities? When might it be more useful to use FTP?

2. What are some of the limitations of Archie as a search tool?

WAIS
Indexes and Databases

C H A P T E R 7

OBJECTIVES

Upon completing the material presented in this chapter, you should understand the following aspects of the Internet:

✦ The concept behind WAIS

✦ How to use the WAIS programs

✦ How to specify WAIS indexes to search

✦ How to do a keyword search

✦ How to construct effective searches using WAIS

✦ How to access WAIS via Gopher

BEFORE YOU START

To perform online exercises in this chapter, you need the following:

✦ An IBM PC compatible running Windows and connected to the Internet

✦ Installed copies of the WinWAIS and WSGopher software on the PC you are using. The versions shown here are WinWAIS 2.4 and WSGopher 1.2.

A WHAT?

Often in your research or everyday life, you want to find a specific scrap of information from a large and unwieldy body of information. You might want to find that one double-fudge-chocolate-o-rama cookie recipe in your favorite cookbook, or locate magazine articles on ancient Phoenician architecture. In these instances, a number of different strategies are useful. You could sit down with a cookbook and all the magazines that you think are relevant, and peruse their tables of contents, looking for likely chapters or titles. This would take you a while, and you might not be able to find what you're looking for just from chapter titles; you might have to page through lots of text to find the exact bit of information.

A more effective strategy is to use an index of the work in question. Most cookbooks and magazines are indexed in some way. The cookbook has an alphabetical listing of genres of cooking, techniques, and specific recipes: You find the name of the recipe in question, and simply turn to the page indicated. There are published indexes for magazines that often index the contents of several related magazines at once: You look for the subject or author in the index, then chase down the indicated articles in the magazine stacks. You know the specific kinds of information for which you are looking, and these indexes tell you how to get to it.

Computers allow large amounts of information to be stored for later retrieval. **WAIS (Wide Area Information System)** provides a method for indexing and accessing specific bodies of knowledge. Anything that you can obtain on the Internet—mail messages, text and electronic books, Usenet articles, computer code, image and graphics files, sound files, e-mail addresses, raw-data databases—WAIS is powerful and flexible enough to **index** and store for later retrieval. It was developed originally as a joint project among Thinking Machines, Inc., Apple Computers, Inc., and two stockbroker firms, Dow Jones and KMPG Peat Marwick. They intended to create methods to allow speedy keyword access to masses of market information being constantly made available. WAIS has evolved to index much more.

HOW DOES WAIS WORK?

WAIS was designed on the client/server model of computer communication. The client/server model requires two programs to utilize WAIS. A WAIS server program is running at several computers that are repositories of WAIS indexes, and WAIS client software is needed in order to access these servers. The WAIS server program runs constantly on its host computer, waiting for requests from WAIS client programs. The many different kinds of WAIS client programs range from desktop computer clients to UNIX clients; they all have the ability to query and receive information from WAIS servers.

The WAIS server is run by the keeper of some store of information, often a large collection of many related items. The cool-photohst WAIS index (stands for cool photography history, not that there also is an uncool-photohst server), for instance, stores all the messages posted to the listserv PHOTOHST, a listserv about the history of photography. Anyone interested in past discussions on PHOTOHST can use that particular WAIS index to search for articles and items.

WAIS indexes are indexed by **keyword**, which means that when a new index is created for a collection of data, WAIS looks through each item, recording the words in each file. This is much more exhaustive than the index of a cookbook, which indexes only recipe names and categories. You wouldn't find an index listing all the occurrences of "flour" in a cookbook. A WAIS index examines each and every word, then decides whether to list it in the database. However, it is smart enough to discard words such as "a," "the," and "I," words that occur so frequently and in so many contexts that it is pointless to index them. When WAIS finishes examining everything, it creates the index and begins waiting for a request.

BOX 7.1	**WHICH WAIS DID HE GO?**

How can you tell which WAIS you have? To date, there are three versions of WAIS index software, each with different capabilities. You will not always know which WAIS you have, but the following covers the three versions with common names and their special capabilities. If you see that the server you are using is of one of these types, you can make use of its functions to the fullest. If you don't see the server identified in any way, you can test out the functions to see what you're dealing with, or simply assume that you're using the oldest version.

Common WAIS, or "b5" WAIS is the original version released by Thinking Machines, Inc. It does not allow Boolean operators. Searches are entered "dogs cats birds," and the server interprets this as "dogs OR cats OR birds."

Indiana University IUBio version adds Boolean operators, but they must be in all capitals for the server to recognize them. A search would be entered: "dogs AND cats AND birds," not "dogs and cats and birds," or the server will look for the word "and" as well.

The freeWAIS version from the Clearinghouse for Network Information Discovery and Retrieval (CNIDR) allows lowercase Boolean operators. In addition to Boolean operators, freeWAIS allows for truncation, the ability to type in the first part of a word (the truncated word), enter an asterisk (*) at the end, and have the WAIS server return all files with words beginning in that manner. Entering "dog*" would return "dog," "dogs," "doggies," "doggedly," and "doggerel."

Unfortunately, not all WAISes are alike. Early versions of the program allow you to search for keywords, but do not allow searches based on multiple keywords using **Boolean operators** (AND, OR, and NOT; see Chapter 4, Box 4.7). In the older software, if you were to enter "dogs cats" as keywords, WAIS would look for documents with the word "dogs" in it, as well as documents with "cats." There was no guarantee that these documents would contain both "dogs" and "cats." In the newer version of the software, you can search for "dogs AND cats," documents with both "dogs" and "cats" somewhere in the file. If you wanted to search for documents that contain "dogs" or "cats," you would search for "dogs OR cats." Here the older version, without Boolean, is assumed.

When you run your WAIS client program, you can access any of the WAIS indexes that the client knows about, or for which it has the computer address. The client program opens a connection with the server you select, sends it the keywords you specify, and receives the information that the server returns. These connections to other computers are rather brief, only long enough to convey the requests and responses. The connection is then closed, the server waits for a new request, and the client helps you process the returns.

WAIS NO TIME!

There are two ways to access WAIS servers: You can use a WAIS client program directly, or find WAIS on such network tools as Gopher and the World Wide Web. The Gopher and WWW access are, in many ways, easier to use because searching and viewing results mimics closely the Gopher and WWW environments. However, WAIS client programs often allow a great deal of flexibility, having more functions than Gopher and WWW access. For example, the Windows client allows you to use **relevance feedback**. You can tell the client, "I really like this article that you found for me, please find me more articles like this one." Unfortunately, not all servers support the added features of this client. As exercises for this chapter, you'll do a short WAIS client session, as well as use some WAIS indexes via Gopher. Although WAIS clients are available on a number of platforms, you will use client software on a PC using Windows. The concepts covered here apply to any platform, whether it be Macintosh, Windows, or a UNIX nongraphical or X user interface.

There are five basic things you need to know: (1) how to start the WAIS client software; (2) how to specify which WAIS servers you'd like to search; (3) how to initiate the search by entering keywords or questions; (4) what to do with the information once you find it; and (5) how to close the program when you are done.

Here's the situation:

You're taking a class on Eastern religions. You're particularly interested in Taoism, on which you'll write your term paper. For now you're only looking for general resources: scholarly forums and newsletters, primary texts, images, and pictures that would be useful.

You'll use WAIS to locate information.

GETTING ON

First you need to access a WAIS client.

 Visually locate the WAIS program icon on the Program Manager window. It should look similar to the one below.

Wais

To start the WAIS program, double-click on the WAIS icon.

A WAIS Query window appears onscreen, similar to the one shown in Figure 7.1.

SELECTING WAIS SERVERS TO SEARCH

The number of generally accessible WAIS servers has now passed the 500 mark. Scrolling through 30 or more screens of WAIS server names to find the desired indexes can be tedious and time-consuming. Rather than listing all 500+ WAIS

FIGURE 7.1

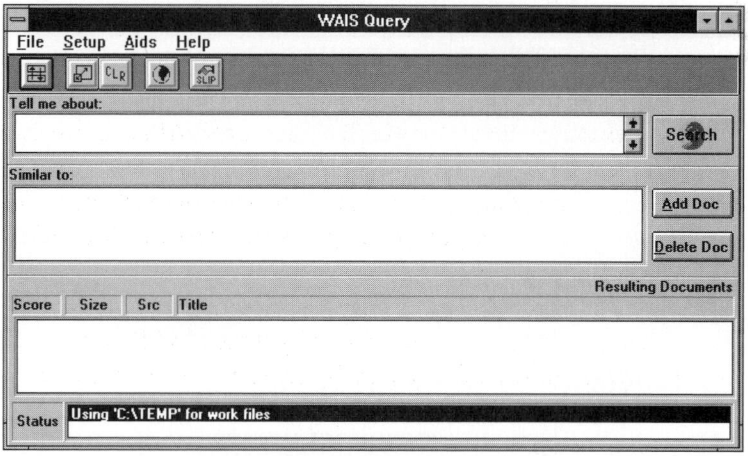

```
WAIS Query
File   Setup   Aids   Help

Tell me about:
                                                              Search

Similar to:
                                                              Add Doc
                                                              Delete Doc

                                            Resulting Documents
Score   Size   Src   Title


Status  Using 'C:\TEMP' for work files
```

servers on the main menu, a Directory of Servers was created, which can be used as a starting point. It is a WAIS index of WAIS indexes that can be searched by keyword to find WAIS servers that are relevant to your search. You need to tell the WAIS program which servers you would like to search, including the Directory of Servers. You can do this from the File menu option Select Sources.

Before starting, however, you need to make sure that the installed copy of the client software on your computer does, indeed, contain the source you need to use.

From the Setup menu, select Sources.

The Sources Editor dialog box is displayed, similar to the one shown in Figure 7.2.

Single-click on DofS Directory of Servers in the Available Sources list box.

The information pertaining to DofS is displayed on the bottom half, similar to Figure 7.3.

If entries displayed onscreen are different from those in Figure 7.3, change them so that they are the same and click on Change.

FIGURE 7.2

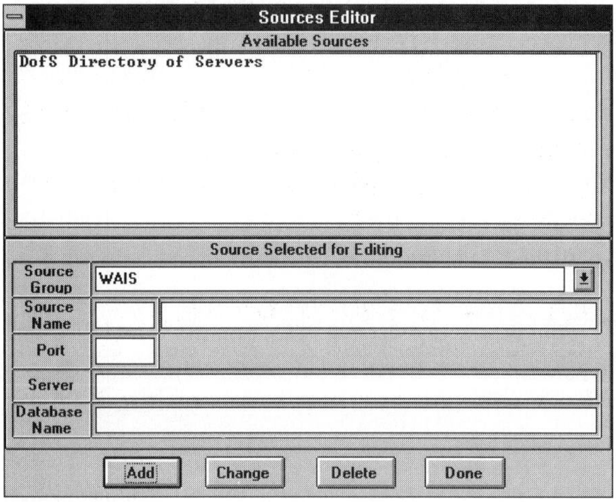

Sources Editor
Available Sources
DofS Directory of Servers

Source Selected for Editing	
Source Group	WAIS
Source Name	
Port	
Server	
Database Name	

[Add] [Change] [Delete] [Done]

FIGURE 7.3

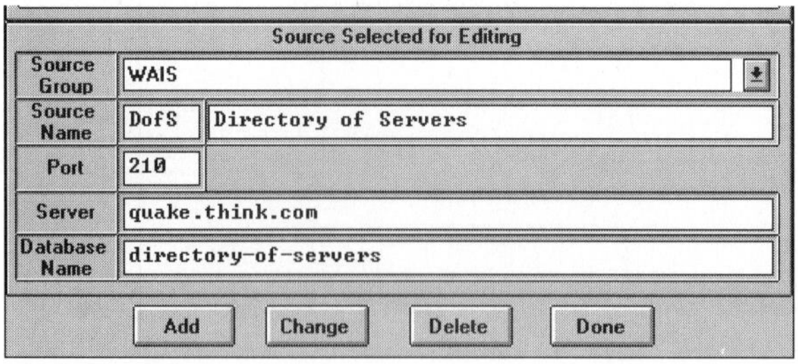

Source Selected for Editing		
Source Group	WAIS	
Source Name	DofS	Directory of Servers
Port	210	
Server	quake.think.com	
Database Name	directory-of-servers	

[Add] [Change] [Delete] [Done]

Click on Done.

The Sources Editor dialog box closes.

Now you are ready to specify sources.

 From the File menu, choose Select Sources.

The WAIS Sources dialog box appears as shown in Figure 7.4.

Make sure that the Source Group text box displays WAIS. If not, click on the down arrow button to the right and select WAIS from the drop-down menu.

Double-click on the DofS Directory of Servers which appears in the lower box.

The DofS Directory of Servers option will be added to the Sources Included in Current Searches box in the upper half of the WAIS Sources box.

Click the Done button at the bottom of the WAIS Sources box.

You are returned to the WAIS Query window.

Now you are ready to locate all those WAIS servers dealing with Eastern religious resources. You need to enter the keywords in the Tell me about: box. WinWAIS allows you to enter your question in **natural language**, or you can simply enter keywords. For example, you could enter "Eastern religions, especially Taoism in Asia," or you could enter simple keywords, like "religion," "Asia," "Taoism," and "Tao." In either case, WinWAIS will try to retrieve sources that contain the significant words.

FIGURE 7.4

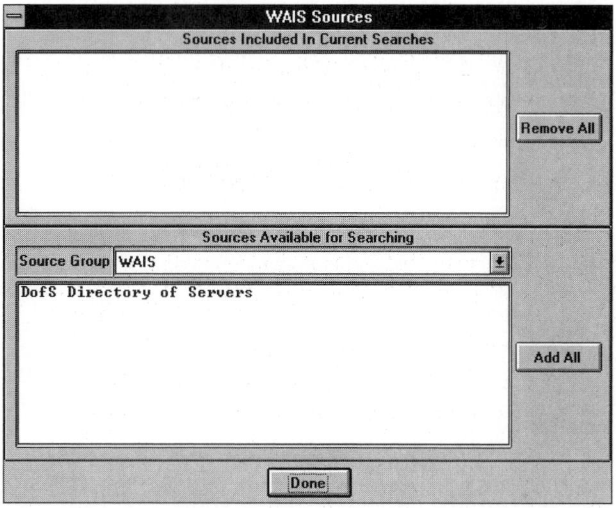

```
┌─────────────────────────────────────────────────┐
│ ─                    WAIS Sources                  │
│          Sources Included In Current Searches      │
│ ┌──────────────────────────────────────┐          │
│ │                                       │          │
│ │                                       │          │
│ │                                       │ ┌───────┐│
│ │                                       │ │Remove All││
│ │                                       │ └───────┘│
│ │                                       │          │
│ └──────────────────────────────────────┘          │
│                                                    │
│            Sources Available for Searching         │
│ Source Group │WAIS                          │ ▼│  │
│ ┌──────────────────────────────────────┐          │
│ │DofS Directory of Servers              │          │
│ │                                       │ ┌───────┐│
│ │                                       │ │Add All ││
│ │                                       │ └───────┘│
│ │                                       │          │
│ └──────────────────────────────────────┘          │
│                    ┌──────┐                        │
│                    │ Done │                        │
│                    └──────┘                        │
└─────────────────────────────────────────────────┘
```

In the Tell me about: text box, enter **religion Asia Taoism Tao**. You don't need to add punctuation.

Click the Search button located to the right of the Tell me about: box or press (ENTER).

The familiar Windows hourglass cursor will appear while WAIS is searching. After a brief pause, a window similar to the one in Figure 7.5 appears.

The Resulting Documents section of the WAIS Query screen shows the results of the search. Note that the status box at the bottom of the screen lists the number of items found. In Figure 7.5, the number is 50.

 Scroll through the list to see the result—that is, the WAIS servers selected.

Notice that there are four columns in the Resulting Documents box. The first column is labeled **Score**. This is the score that WAIS uses to rank the return. WAIS counts the number of times a particular resource matches the keywords you specified. The one with the most hits gets the highest score, four stars, and appears at the top of the list. WAIS is guessing which one will be of most value to you.

In the next column is the size of the resource in bytes. *2K* means 2 kilobytes. This may not mean much to you right now, as the listing you are looking at is that of WAIS servers. When you find a resource document you want to retrieve, the information on size may be of interest to you.

The third column, labeled Src, lists the source (WAIS server) in which the document was found. In this case they were all from DofS, since the only source which you queried was the Directory of Servers.

As you look at the titles listed, you may find some to be quite cryptic. (However, .src at the end indicates that they are searchable WAIS files.) You might

FIGURE 7.5

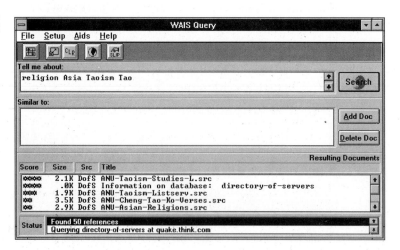

BOX 7.2

WHERE *IS* THAT DIRECTORY OF SERVERS?

If you are having trouble connecting to the Directory of Servers, it may be that your client is set to look at one of the popular Directory of Servers which sometimes is not accessible. You may get a nasty-looking "socket error" if this is the case. There are a couple of other WAIS servers you can use instead. All you need to do is to change the Server name in the Sources Editor dialog box (see Figure 7.3) to one of the following:

wais.wais.com	192.216.46.98
cnidr.org	128.109.179.4

notice that some items do not actually contain any of your keywords in the title. It's easy to understand why ANU-Asian-Religions.src is included, but how did Tantric-News.src get included? Why did WAIS return these? The search was conducted based on the introduction files for each server. So if an introduction file contained these keywords, WAIS selected it.

Let's specify a WAIS index that will be used for your search. There are a lot of extraneous WAIS servers listed. You need take only the ones you want; you can choose one or several to search simultaneously. ANU-Asian-Religions.src seems to be a natural choice, but let's look at its introduction files.

Double-click on ANU-Asian-Religions.src in the Resulting Documents list box.

The hourglass cursor will appear for a moment, and you will be presented with a dialog box containing information about this particular resource, as shown in Figure 7.6.

The introduction file is displayed in the upper half of the window. It may tell you what version of WAIS is being used, when the file was last updated, and what keywords are associated with the file. You can scroll through the file to determine whether this source contains material relevant to your search. You can even highlight keywords in the document.

From the Edit menu, select Find Key or press the (F5) function key.

Keywords are now highlighted in the introduction file.

Find Key is a toggle command. That is, keywords will be highlighted in all documents you view until you enter the command again. If, after reading the introduction file, you feel that this source would be worth searching, you can add it to the list of Sources Available for Searching.

Click on the Add This Source button.

The button goes dim.

FIGURE 7.6

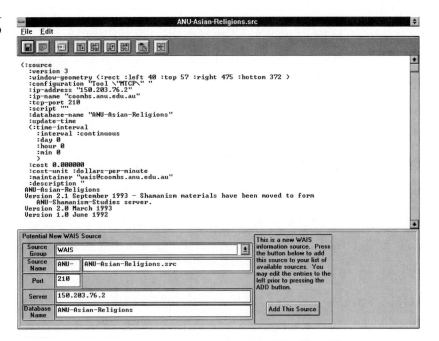

From the File menu choose Done or press the (F3) function key.

You return to the WAIS Query window.

Similarly, select ANU-Taoism-Listserv.src (and any other sources) for use.

Now you need to specify sources you will use for the next search.

From the File Menu, choose Select Sources.

The WAIS Sources dialog box appears, similar to Figure 7.7.

Double-click the items you wish to select for searching.

The items appear in the Sources Included in Current Searches box.

You have now selected a few additional sources to search, but you have not removed the original Directory of Servers source. Since you no longer are in need of this resource, you can remove it from the list.

Double-click the Directory of Servers listed in the Sources Included in Current Searches box.

It is removed from the Sources Included in Current Searches box. Your WAIS Sources box should now look similar to the one shown in Figure 7.8.

Click the Done button at the bottom of the WAIS Sources box.

The dialog box disappears and you are returned to the WAIS Query menu.

FIGURE 7.7

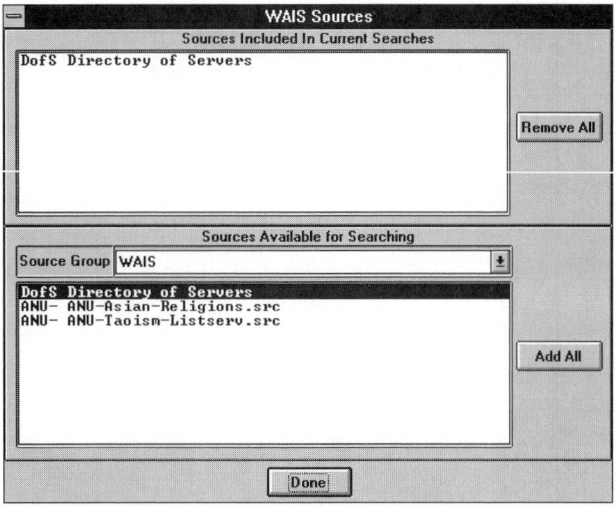

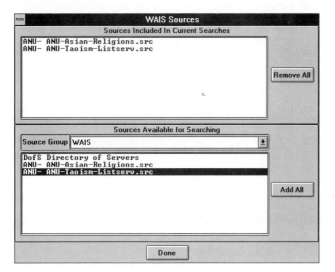

FIGURE 7.8

SEARCH USING KEYWORDS

Up to now, you were determining and selecting which WAIS indexes you want to search. You are now ready for the actual search for documents. You did something similar to this just a bit earlier in selecting the servers. You can use the same keywords as before, or you may wish to use more specific words. Carefully choosing keywords can help improve the relevance of the materials retrieved. If, for example, you search the word "Taoism" in a server called Taoism listserv, you

BOX 7.3	**KEYING UP**

When we want to get specific in our searching, we need to choose our keywords carefully. A general term may return a huge volume of mostly irrelevant files. An inappropriate or rare term may not return anything at all. When looking for information about a topic in a database, it is often appropriate to use keywords that are specific and narrow. For instance, the keyword "Bible" will certainly get us a lot of returns in indexes. But if we know more precisely what we seek, we should use words related to it to narrow the search. For example, "Pentateuch Exodus Moses Sinai" will give whatever returns in the WAIS index that contains these specific words. This will get you closer to the information that you want faster.

If you don't find the sought-after information in your first attempt, try again with different, related words. If after a few attempts, using different synonyms and related words, you don't succeed in getting any returns, this WAIS index (or indeed any database you're searching) may not contain information on your topic. This is a sign that it is time to move on to a different index or resource that more closely matches your search topic.

will most likely get thousands of hits. You will need to be more specific in your searching. Think about what facets of Eastern religions and Taoism interest you. You might search words like Veda, Buddha, Tao Te Ching, jain, and so on. You want to see what kinds of documents on your specific topic you can retrieve from these sources, and how important they might be.

 Delete your previous keywords from the Tell me about: text box and replace them with **buddha, veda**. You don't need to add punctuation.

Click on the Search button or press ⌴ENTER⌴.

The familiar Windows hourglass cursor will appear while WAIS is searching.

There should be a (possibly long) pause, during which the hourglass cursor remains and the bottom of the screen flashes status messages about searching each database individually (each is probably on a different computer, remember). When the WinWAIS client finishes querying all the servers you have chosen to search, a window similar to the one in Figure 7.9 appears.

NOTE:	If any of the servers that you try to query are unavailable, you may receive a rather annoying "socket error" message. Simply click the OK box, and WAIS will continue onto the next server selected for searching.

FIGURE 7.9

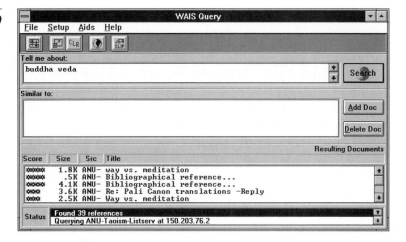

The results of the search will appear in the Resulting Documents box in the lower half of the screen. Note that the number of items found is displayed in the status box at the bottom of the screen. In Figure 7.9, the number is 39.

There may have actually been 39 documents with these keywords, or it may be that WinWAIS is set to retrieve only 39 documents. The maximum number of documents WinWAIS will return to you is set in the Setup menu, under the Max Documents limit option. The default setting is 75. Since WAIS attempts to sort documents by their relevance to your topic, it is unlikely that you would want to raise this number. You may, however, wish to lower it. Remember, not all of these hits are going to be relevant. You need to look for titles that look interesting and briefly look at the content. This may take a while, but a lot of the entries you can write off immediately. For example, those that seem to be conversation subject

BOX 7.4   NEW AIRPORT IN MEXICO?

Even with the good keywords and Boolean operators, some queries will retrieve many false hits. Take, for example, a search for airports in the state of New Mexico. You might get many hits with the words "new" and "mexico" that don't deal with New Mexico! What you really need to search for is the word "new" next to the word "mexico." The **adjacency operator** (adj) can do this for you. Some WAIS servers support this feature, which means doing the search "new adj Mexico" should retrieve only documents in which "new" occurs next to "Mexico." Of course, you may still get hits with things like "looking at what's new, Mexico announces another airport," but the use of adjacency operators can often vastly improve the relevance of your search hits.

lines or those that don't relate to your topic can be eliminated immediately. As you look at the titles that are listed, you may find them to be quite cryptic. Sometimes all the titles will be similar, and it is impossible to tell the content without opening the document. You might notice that some items do not actually contain any of your keywords in the title. WAIS returned these because the keywords were somewhere in the document, not necessarily in the title of the document.

Scroll through the list to see the results.

As you scroll through the list, double-click on an item that looks interesting.

A window appears displaying the contents of the file.

As you view the document, you can view the document listed before or after this one by opening the <u>E</u>dit menu and selecting View <u>n</u>ext document or View <u>p</u>rev document. When you find a document that may be of value, you can save it to a file on your local computer or print it. These commands are found in the File menu.

When you are done viewing documents, you can exit the document viewer from the File menu or by pressing the F3 function key.

Exit the document viewer by opening the <u>F</u>ile menu and selecting <u>D</u>one or pressing the F3 function key.

You are returned to the WAIS Query window.

You seem to have found a number of things relating to your topic, Taoism within Eastern Religions. These include:

✦ Irrelevant drivel

✦ Usenet and listserv articles (for a more detailed discussion of these two, see Chapter 2, on listservs, and Chapter 3, on Usenet), including everything from factual information, scholarly discussion, rants, and out-and-out flame wars

✦ Reviews of books or other documents

✦ Pointers, references, or annotations to documents not present here

✦ Some actual documents that relate to your Eastern religions topic, containing useful facts or theories

This, like most Internet resources, will require a bit of weeding and patience on your part. You can skip those that at first glance appear to be irrelevant, and skim through the rest looking for anything that might be useful.

Especially with the archives of Usenet and listserv discussions, you may be able to make contacts through the Internet to people knowledgeable about the subject matter. The author's e-mail address will generally be included in a given

BOX 7.5

GIVE ME MORE LIKE THIS!

One of the nice features of WinWAIS is the concept of *relevance feedback*. You can tell WAIS which articles were actually on your topic and ask it to find other documents similar to it. You can do this by dragging relevant search result titles from the Resulting Documents box into the Similar to: box and running your search again. WAIS doesn't actually understand the concepts in your question, but it does pick up additional keywords from the documents. Note that not all WAIS servers support this feature, so you may or may not get improved results, but it's always worth a try!

message; if the author seems to know significant details of your topic, you can attempt correspondence with an e-mail message explaining who you are, what you are looking for, and how you came across his or her name.

CLOSING THE WAIS QUERY SCREEN

Close the WAIS Query Screen and exit the program by opening the File menu and selecting Exit.

A dialog box will appear asking you if you are sure that you wish to exit the program.

Click OK.

The program closes.

GOPHERING WAIS

As an example of a different client, you'll delve briefly into using WAIS indexes from Gopher. It is a bit different from the WinWAIS client, but the basic idea is the same. You will attempt the same search, looking for items on Eastern religions.

Start your Gopher client by double-clicking on the WSGopher icon: .
From the File menu, select New Gopher Item or press (CTRL)-**N**.

You have two ways to connect.

✦ The first is to Gopher to gopher-gw.micro.umn.edu, port 70. The Gopher menu is displayed with just one option, WAISes. Select it.

✦ The second method is to Gopher to gopher2.tc.umn.edu, then select Other Gopher and Information Servers. You can then scroll down to select WAIS Based Information.

Use one of the methods above to connect to the WAISes.

Regardless of which route you took, a screen similar to the one in Figure 7.10 is displayed.

NOTE: The title bar differs depending on the route.

In this menu, the List of all WAIS Sources will give you a list of all the WAIS sources available at this site. This time, instead of scrolling through the list, you will search the Directory of WAIS Servers to locate servers on your topic. You'll want to open WAIS Databases sorted by Letter, because it contains the Directory of WAIS servers option.

Select WAIS Databases sorted by Letter, and then Directory of WAIS servers.

The Select Extra View dialog box appears.

Click on Directory English (US) and click OK.

A screen similar to the one shown in Figure 7.11 is displayed.

Enter the words you used earlier to describe your topic—**asia religion taoism tao**—then click Search.

After a pause, you should see a new menu with some familiar titles, similar to the one shown in Figure 7.12.

These returns should look familiar. Most likely the servers you chose to search will be listed here, in addition to several others on the topic.

FIGURE 7.10

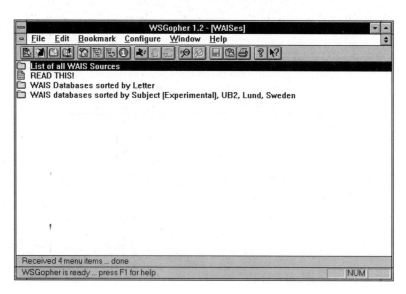

FIGURE 7.11

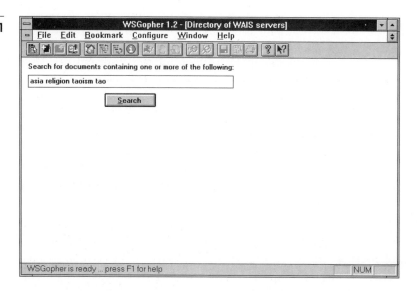

FIGURE 7.12

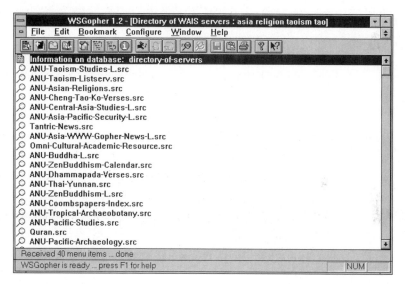

The drawback of using Gopher as a WAIS client is this: You must now search each WAIS index that looks relevant individually, whereas with WinWAIS you can simply drag each one that you think is relevant into the In these sources box. There is the advantage of the relatively easy-to-use and perhaps more familiar Gopher interface. Actually searching the indexes is left as an exercise.

 When you are satisfied, exit Gopher.

SUMMARY

In this chapter, many of the terms and concepts that are necessary to use WAIS are introduced:

✦ WAIS (Wide Area Information System) provides a method for indexing and accessing resources on the Internet.

✦ In order to utilize WAIS, you must have access to WAIS client software.

✦ You need to tell WAIS which WAIS server you'd like to search for information. Once that is specified, you just enter keywords and WAIS will return all the documents that match your search criteria.

✦ Once a desired document is located, you can view it onscreen. You can then print it or save it on the local computer if you wish.

✦ WAIS can also be accessed through the Gopher or WWW.

KEY TERMS

adjacency operator	index	score
Boolean operators	natural language	WAIS (Wide Area
keyword	relevance feedback	Information System)

REVIEW QUESTIONS

1. What is the purpose of WAIS?

2. Why is it useful to search the Directory of servers source first?

3. How do you tell WAIS that you want to search a specific index?

4. How do you view an introduction file for a WAIS index?

5. What are some uses for the introduction file for a WAIS index?

6. What does the score on the WAIS search Results screen mean?

7. Explain the concept of adjacency in searching and why might you use it.

8. What are your options once you locate a desired document?

9. How do you access WAIS from Gopher?

10. Are there differences between accessing WAIS from a WAIS client and from a Gopher? Explain.

EXERCISES

1. Locate the WAIS index that contains U.S. government documents, specifically health care-related. Specify the location and what it contains.

2. Locate collections of documents about PCs available via WAIS.

3. Often listservs and Usenet are archived with WAIS. Find as many such WAIS indexes as you can.

4. How many vegan and vegetarian recipes involving potatoes can you find using only WAIS indexes?

DISCUSSION TOPICS

1. Think of topics about which you may have to write a term paper, and discuss keywords that might be used when conducting a WAIS search.

2. What are some Internet skills you need before you can effectively use resources found through the WAIS search?

WORLD WIDE WEB (NETSCAPE)
Bringing It All Together

CHAPTER **8**

OBJECTIVES

Upon completing the material presented in this chapter, you should understand the following aspects of the Internet:

✦ The concept behind World Wide Web (WWW)

✦ How to use WWW

✦ How to start a WWW client

✦ How to open a Uniform Resource Locator (URL)

✦ How to find information on a specific topic

✦ How to perform subject-oriented searches in WWW

✦ How to perform index searches in the WWW

BEFORE YOU START

In order to perform online exercises in this chapter, you need the following:

✦ An IBM PC compatible running Windows and connected to the Internet

✦ Installed copy of the WWW client Netscape on the machine you are using. The version of the software shown here is 1.1N.

BRINGING IT ALL TOGETHER

You may be asking: "Bringing it all together? Didn't we already do that? Isn't that what Gopher is for?" Well, yes and no. Yes, Gopher does tie together text documents, Telnet sessions, sounds, graphics, file transfers, and more in an easy-to-use menu-driven format. But the World Wide Web (WWW) takes Gopher one step further by using **hypertext**.

What is hypertext? A hypertext document is a document that not only contains information, but also contains references, or **links**, to other documents that contain information related to the topic at hand. Astute observers should realize that this idea isn't new: It's footnotes! Just as footnotes and bibliographies contain references to other books and articles that deal with whatever you may be reading about, hypertext links are really just references to other documents.

The big difference? When you find a reference in a book, you usually need to go elsewhere to find the reference, if you can find it at all. In a hypertext document, you simply click on the link, and, *bam!* It's there. Not just the name of the author and the title, but the document itself is displayed (given clear weather and fair networking conditions, of course).

How does this compare to Gopher? The two systems do have many similarities—they both organize previously unrelated information, provide ways to navigate across the network easily, and make it possible to access many different types of information (such as text, pictures, sounds, and movies). The important difference is that a Gopher document is only inert text. In Gopher, after viewing a document, you can only go back to the Gopher menu to start on another search path through the menu system. In hypertext documents, upon viewing a document, you can access different links pointing to relevant documents and items.

BOX 8.1	**HYPERTEXT ON THE INTERNET**

HYPERTEXT ON THE INTERNET

In late 1989, there was a proposal by the CERN High-Energy Physics Lab in Switzerland: Why not develop a system to take advantage of computer networking, to allow researchers to share information with each other? There was already a huge amount of data in the lab, but navigating the data was not always easy. You might, for instance, be reading a report that refers to a different set of data somewhere else. To find that data, you would probably have to jump through several hoops with some other program, first finding, then retrieving the desired information. Once you had finally found the information, it was often hard to keep track of it for later reference.

The project had much in common with the Gopher project of the University of Minnesota. The project's aim was to provide a single interface to many

Continued on next page

BOX 8.1

HYPERTEXT ON THE INTERNET (*continued*)

different kinds of information, and to link them together. The approach of the CERN proposal—the World Wide Web proposal—did not call for Gopher-style menus, but instead involved a concept called *hypertext*.

Hypertext has its roots in a 1945 article in the *Atlantic* called "As We May Think," by Vannevar Bush. In the article, Bush describes a machine which he calls a "memex" (and which has turned out to be an accurate prediction for the computers of today). The article predicts that the challenge facing us is no longer to make new discoveries, but instead to make sense of the huge amount of knowledge we already have. A memex would be like a secretary, storing information, and more importantly, storing connections between pieces of information. By making connections—associations—among related ideas and information, the memex could help you find the specific information you were looking for. You would simply start with a related concept, and follow the most promising trail until you came to what you needed!

The word *hypertext* was not coined until the late 1960s by Ted Nelson. Nelson was fascinated by the machine described by Bush, and wrote a pair of books, *Computer Lib* and *Dream Machines*, which laid out in great detail how Nelson saw the future of computers and the future of hypertext. Nelson's vision of hypertext has yet to be realized (he continues to work on Xanadu, which he first proposed in *Dream Machines*), but some claim that the World Wide Web comes awfully close.

So what, then, was the fate of that 1989 proposal at CERN? As you may well have guessed, the proposal was approved, and construction was soon underway on the software to support this scheme. By late 1991, software was available to the Internet community and the Web was born. However, it wasn't until 1993 that the Web began to really take off, with the development of some really slick browsers, including Mosaic. In the few years since then, the Web has seen explosive development, especially from commercial entities. The Netscape browser described in this chapter is the product of this development, one of the first in a new breed of Internet tools developed by companies rather than research and educational institutions.

HOW DOES IT WORK?

The **Web**, as WWW is referred to by Internet users, is based around a client/server model. When you use the Web, you are using two programs, the client and the server. The **client** program, often referred to as a **browser**, is the program running on your local terminal, whether it be a PC, Macintosh, or a UNIX station. It displays information on screen, takes your keystrokes and your mouse clicks, and retrieves the information that you request. It retrieves the information from the **server**. The server program runs on a computer system that provides the Web information: It sits about, waiting for an information request. Upon such a request, it handily provides the requested information to the browser.

For the most part, you need only worry about half of this equation—how the client program works. It is the program you will be using, and everything that has to do with servers should be transparent to you. In the course of using the Web, you will probably be handed off to dozens of different servers on the Internet. The only reason for you to understand what is going on in the background is so that when some documents you request are mysteriously unavailable, you understand that this usually means you attempted to access a server that wasn't working.

The Web deals in a wide variety of information. The most common documents on the Web are written in a form called **HyperText Mark-up Language (HTML)**. Documents are marked up in this format, meaning that codes for formatting and

---

BOX 8.2

WINDOWS CLIENTS FOR THE WORLD WIDE WEB

Several clients are available for the World Wide Web under Windows. The following are the three most popular.

Mosaic for Windows

Mosaic is the first WWW browser, developed by the National Center for Supercomputing Applications. Available via FTP at ftp.ncsa.uiuc.edu, in the directory /PC/Windows/Mosaic.

WinWeb

WinWeb is a browser produced by EINet. At last check, this browser is still in "alpha," which means that it isn't very stable yet. However, by the time this book comes out, it may well be a finished product. Available via FTP at ftp.einet.net, in the directory /einet/pc/winweb.

Netscape for Windows

This browser looks and feels much like Mosaic, but adds many new and exciting features. It is too early to tell, but Netscape may well supplant Mosaic as the browser of choice. However, Netscape Communications is a commercial company, and while the browser is free for educational use, it is not free to the general public. Available via FTP at ftp.netscape.com, in the directory /pub/netscape/windows.

For a current (and more extensive) list of browsers available, you can also turn to the Web itself—a list is available online at http://www.yahoo.com/Computers/World_Wide_Web/Browsers/.

linking are inserted into the text. Each client program interprets the codes differently, depending on the limitations of the platform it is serving. A fancy graphics workstation has more graphics and formatting capabilities than a text-based dumb terminal. With the appropriate client software, you can take full advantage of the display capability of the platform. In any platform, the same text and links will be present, just presented (and formatted) in a different way.

Aside from the hypertext document, you can utilize almost all Internet tools through the Web. It can deal with FTP, Gopher, WAIS, newsgroups, and Telnet sessions. This is a comforting thought—the skills you've acquired elsewhere will now serve you well here. However, the Web also has its own set of skills for you to learn and use.

One thing to note: In WWW, a document is often referred to as a **page**. We will use the terms interchangeably.

USING THE WEB

To use the Web, you need to know how to do the following: (1) start a WWW client program; (2) recognize and select links; (3) follow the link; (4) go back to previous pages; (5) specify a Uniform Resource Locator (URL) to open; and (6) quit WWW.

The Web client program you are using here is Netscape, a program developed by Netscape Communications Corporation. Netscape is a commercial program, but it is free to academic users (including students like yourself!). Netscape is a very popular entry into the WWW browser arena, providing hypertext integrated with multimedia.

We have already claimed that World Wide Web represents the integration of many different kinds of Internet resources. To practice using WWW, it is only fitting that we choose a discipline of the same complexity, and what could that be? Why, history, of course—an area which is a little bit of political science, a little bit of sociology, a little bit of philosophy, and a whole lot of the expression of the liberal arts curriculum.

The question, then, is:

Investigate the causes and effects of the 1917 Russian Bolshevik revolution. Specifically, find out who participated in it, why they did so, and what they did once they gained power.

Start by bringing up your client.

 Visually locate the Netscape program icon in the Program Manager window. It should look similar to the one below.

To start Netscape, double-click on the Netscape icon.

*The **home page**, or opening screen, for a Web server is displayed, as shown in Figure 8.1.*

NOTE: If you see the icon 🖾, a graphic is behind it. If your computer has enough memory, Netscape will automatically load the graphic. If not, you will need to click the Images button in the Netscape toolbar, which will load all of the images in the page you are currently looking at.

This is the home page for the Web at Willamette University. Most documents on the Web will look like this, or at least share certain similarities. The most important similarity will be the existence of links—which, in Netscape, are indicated by <u>underlined</u> text. These links allow you to navigate. By following a link, you will be taken to another page, or to another part of the page you are already looking at.

As you can see in Figure 8.1, Netscape provides several shortcuts for exploring the Internet. Immediately below the menu is a series of buttons called the *toolbar*. The toolbar allows you to do things like move back to a previous document, find text in the document you are currently in, or return to the home page from which you started. Below this, your current location is displayed, in the form of a **Uniform Resource Locator (URL)** (see Box 8.3). Finally, the Directory Buttons are displayed, including buttons like What's New!, Net Search, and Net Directory.

FIGURE 8.1

Toolbar ——————

Current location ——————

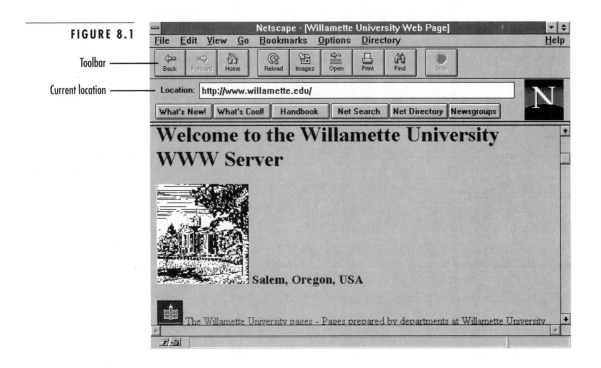

NOTE: Your screen may or may not show the toolbar, the Location, and Directory buttons. If not, open the Options menu and click on these items so that a checkmark appears in front of each.

If you want to quit at any time, you do what you do with any Windows application: From the File menu, select Exit. On the other hand, if you want to select and follow a link, click on it *once*.

 Click on a link.

You are taken to a new page.

Now, if you select a link in the new page, you will progress even further. You can also go back to previously visited pages by clicking on the Back button (labeled with an arrow pointing left) found just under the menu bar.

 Continue to follow links until you have visited three or four pages.

Now, open the Go menu.

The menu shows the titles from all the Web pages you have visited, similar to the one shown in Figure 8.2.

The checkmark in front of a listing indicates that this is the current page on display. When you click on the Back button, you proceed to the page that's listed beneath the current one. The Forward button takes you to the page that's listed just above the current one. The Home button takes you back to the original home page. Furthermore, you can go to any page listed by dragging the mouse to select it.

SUBJECT-ORIENTED CATALOGS OF INFORMATION

Perhaps the best way to start looking for information is to take advantage of the work that other people have already done. Just as Gopher has subject trees, the

FIGURE 8.2

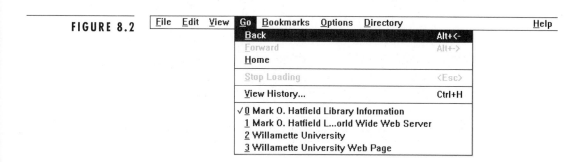

BOX 8.3	# URL

The client you are using needs to know only what format and protocol to expect of the desired information, and it retrieves it by that protocol. The user or Web author specifies the format and protocol by using an appropriate Uniform Resource Locator (URL). URLs are a relatively new standard for specifying any kind of information on the Internet, and though they may at first seem cryptic, they are really very simple.

A URL usually specifies three things: *<method>://<host computer>/ <pathname>*.

✦ *<method>* is the general kind of protocol or method to use to retrieve the document: gopher for Gopher documents and directories; ftp for FTP; http for HTML documents on the Web; news for Usenet newsgroups; and telnet for Telnet sessions.

✦ *<host computer>* refers to the specific computer at which the information is located. For example, Gopher, FTP, and HTML documents all have a server on a specific host computer. Telnet sessions have a specific destination computer. Newsgroups are the only exception—instead of a hostname, you provide a newsgroup (for example, news:news.answers).

✦ *<pathname>* refers to where (such as Gopher or FTP or HTML) the information is to be found (newsgroups and Telnet sessions don't have this).

The following are some fictitious examples of URLs and explanations.

✦ http://www.willamette.edu/webdev/wumap—An HTML document wumap from the computer www.willamette.edu in the directory webdev.

✦ ftp://ftp.whatsa.matta.u.edu/games/silly/eggo.Z—An FTP file eggo.Z at the computer ftp.whatsa.matta.u.edu in the directory /games/silly.

✦ gopher://gopher.burrow.com/00/interesting/stuff—The Gopher file stuff (we know it's a file because of the two zeros there; the numbers refer to the Gopher item type) at the Gopher server at gopher.burrow.com in the directory /interesting/stuff.

Once you get the hang of them, they are not hard to understand at all.

It is possible to use URLs to jump directly to a document without navigating there using links. For that reason, descriptions of available Web resources are often accompanied by a URL. Using Netscape, for example, this can be accomplished by opening the File menu, selecting Open Location, and specifying the URL.

World Wide Web has "virtual libraries" and subject-oriented collections of pointers to information available on the Web.

You will use the Directory Buttons to get to a starting point for finding information. Netscape's several buttons provide quick access to directories of Internet resources. These directories are maintained by Netscape Communications, and provide pointers to other, more comprehensive directories.

Click on the Net Directory button in the Directory Buttons.

Netscape's Internet Directory, similar to the one shown in Figure 8.3, appears.

NOTE: As this book was going to press, the Net Directory listed three resources on the opening screen: Yahoo, World Wide Web Servers, and Virtual Tourist. This may change by the time you read this, but the reference to Yahoo should be easy to find. If you have any trouble, you can go directly to Yahoo using the method described in Box 8.3. The URL for Yahoo is http://www.yahoo.com/.

Click on Yahoo.

The Yahoo page, similar to the one shown in Figure 8.4, is displayed.

Yahoo is a directory of Internet resources. One of Yahoo's outstanding features is that users may add new topics and resources to the lists, which means that (in a sense) Yahoo is maintained by the Internet community. Topics in

FIGURE 8.3

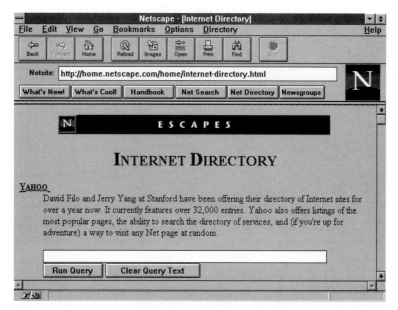

FIGURE 8.4

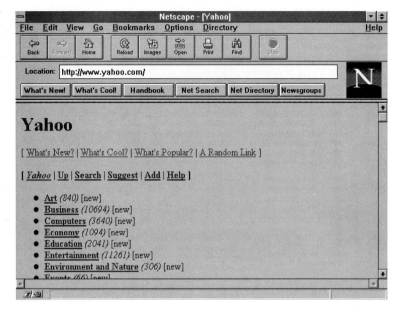

Yahoo range from art to computers to politics. And, fortunately for your purposes, they also include history.

You might notice that History is not among the topics listed, but Humanities is. And, as any good liberal arts student can tell you, history is one of the humanities.

Find and select the link Humanities.

The Humanities list appears, similar to the one shown in Figure 8.5.

Notice that each topic listing includes links to further subtopics, such as history, and to resources relating to that topic. The number in parentheses after some subtopics indicates the number of entries in that subtopic. If the listing is a resource, you can view it by selecting it; no number follows it.

Follow History.

You'll be taken to the Yahoo listing of History resources.

Find and follow Index - History - WWW Virtual Library.

You'll be taken to the Virtual Library history resource screen, similar to the one shown in Figure 8.6.

You'll browse this page to find some information.

Follow the link Alphabetical list of history resources.

You'll be provided with the Full Index of Available Resources, similar to the one shown in Figure 8.7.

FIGURE 8.5

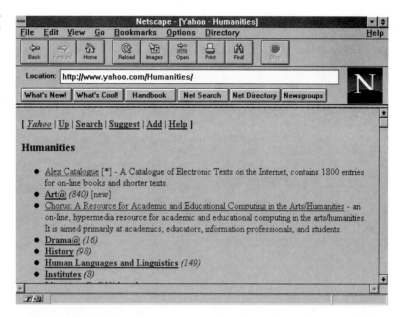

FIGURE 8.6

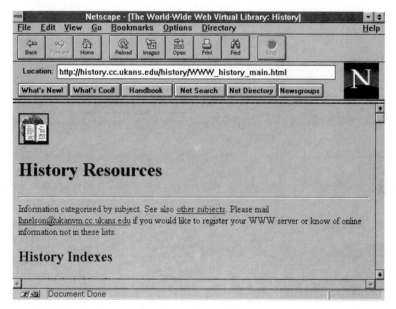

A lot of items are listed here. Normally, you'd actually read through this list, scanning for what seemed appropriate, but for now we'll point you in the right direction.

Since this is a long page, scrolling through the screen can take some time. One way to speed this up is to use the Find... command in the Edit menu. You

FIGURE 8.7

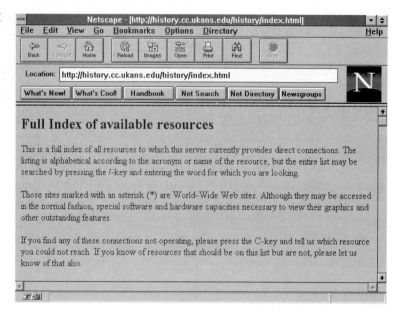

will use this to find the word "malin" (the name of the site we're looking for). The search is not case-sensitive, meaning that you can use both uppercase and lowercase when entering the text for which to search.

   From the Edit menu, select the Find... command or press (CTRL)-**F.**

Netscape will prompt you to enter a search string.

Type **malin** in the Find What text box and click Find Next or press (ENTER).
Click on the Cancel button to close the Find dialog box.

The following text is found:

MALIN: Historical Archives (ftp ukanaix.cc.ukans.edu cd pub\history) (US)

Follow MALIN: Historical Archives.

You'll be connected to the Malin FTP site, as indicated by a screen similar to Figure 8.8.

Two things to notice here: The first is that this is an actual FTP site, whatever that means. On the Web, it really doesn't matter. The second is that this FTP site looks like everything else on the Web. In fact, there seems to be no difference between one kind of service and another.

   Find and follow Europe files.

You'll be presented with different categories of European history.

FIGURE 8.8

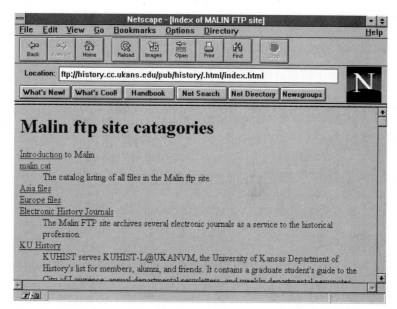

You've successfully used a subject-oriented index to find information relevant to your question. Congratulations! You can follow vsmith2.art to display it onscreen.

Find and follow Modern European History.

You'll be given the choice of several different nationalities—including Russian.

Find and follow Russian History.

At the time this book was going to press, the following article was listed:

vsmith2.art Three Men in Russia: Marye, Robins, and Francis, 1914–18, by Valentine M. Smith

You've successfully used a subject-oriented index to find information relevant to your question. Congratulations! You can follow vsmith2.art to display it onscreen.

Follow vsmith2.art.

The document is loaded and displayed.

Looking over it, you should notice that it is an overview of the period of the revolution, analyzing the perspectives of Americans in Moscow. Not perfectly suited, but still an excellent match. If you want this document printed, you know what to do: From the File menu, select Print. You can also save the document to disk on your machine by opening the File menu and selecting Save as... or pressing (CTRL)-S. You will be prompted for a filename and location to put the file.

BOX 8.4

SEARCHABLE WEB INDEXES

The WWW has gained many keyword-based searchable indexes since the first edition of this book. Some are listed below, along with their URLs.

✦ ALIWEB (Archie-Like Indexing for the Web)
URL: http://web.nexor.co.uk/aliweb/doc/aliweb.html

ALIWEB employs an interesting technique—each participating site maintains a list of documents which it would like indexed, including short descriptions of the documents, and keywords by which the documents can be found. The contents of ALIWEB are also included in the W3Catalog.

✦ The World Wide Web Worm (WWWW)
URL: http://www.cs.colorado.edu/home/mcbryan/WWWW.html

This is one of the first indexes which used "worming" through the Web—following link after link after link automatically in an attempt to find many documents—to generate an index of documents. You can search for documents by their titles, or by the text which cites those documents in other documents (the text that you click on in a link).

✦ The WebCrawler
URL: http://www.webcrawler.cs.washington.edu/WebCrawler.WebQuery.html

The WebCrawler is like the World Wide Web Worm, except that it indexes the whole text of the document instead of just the title. This is helpful when other search engines don't turn up what you seek. For instance, if you're looking for information on euphonium valves, and the information is buried in a document entitled "A History of Brass." Only an index which includes the entire text of the document will unearth the right answer for you.

✦ Lycos
URL: http://lycos.cs.cmu.edu/

Lycos is one of our personal favorites. A recent entry, it operates much like the WebCrawler. However, it tries to automatically generate an abstract of the document in question, so that you can try to determine whether the document is appropriate before you spend time trying to retreive it. The abstracts are computer-generated, so they're not the most readable in the world—but the Internaut who needs even more sophistication in search tools will find this one invaluable.

A longer and more current list of searchable indexes is available via the Web itself, at http://cuiwww.unige.ch/meta-index.html.

KEYWORD-ORIENTED INDEXES

Another way to find information on a specific subject is through an index. In a book, an index helps you find specific information quickly, without messing around with the table of contents to try to figure out which chapter the information might be in. Similarly, indexes on the Web allow you to use specific **keywords** to find the information you seek. You will do this from a searchable index called the W3Catalog.

To get to the W3Catalog, you will use Net Search, another of the Directory Buttons. Similar to the Net Directory button, this is a prepared index of Internet resources which help you to search for information online.

Click on the Net Search button.

Netscape's Internet Search page appears, similar to the one shown in Figure 8.9

Find the text SEARCH ENGINE SEARCH.

Follow W3 SEARCH ENGINES.

Find the text: List-based WWW Catalogs.

Follow CUI World Wide Web Catalog.

The W3 Catalog main page appears, similar to the one shown in Figure 8.10.

FIGURE 8.9

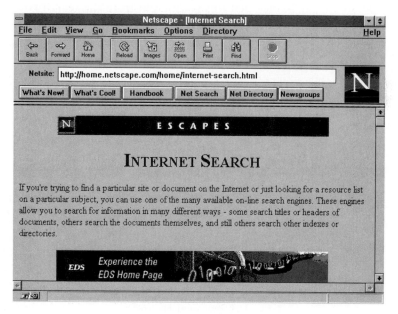

FIGURE 8.10

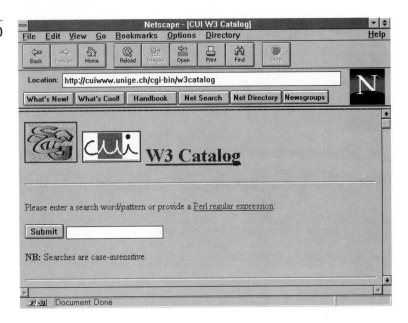

The W3 Catalog indexes several collections of information about what is on the Internet. The W3 Catalog allows you to search the contents of all of these indexes by allowing you to provide keywords and returning a list of all items that match. Notice that this is different from the search you did earlier, where you searched for text within a page. This time, you'll be searching a database, and will get back a completely new page based on the keywords you supply. In this case, you will search on the keyword "soviet."

 Click on the Submit text box. When the blinking cursor appears, type **soviet** and click the Submit button.

Scroll down this screen, if necessary, until you see the following text: result of search for "soviet":. A list of resources having to do with "soviet" will be displayed. Scroll further down the screen and you will see the following.

August 5, 1993: The University of North Carolina at Chapel Hill now has a Web server. Interesting documents include the UNC Virtual Museum (which currently contains a hypermedia version of the Library of Congress Soviet Archives Exhibit and a Mathematical Art Gallery) and more. (nwn)

Follow the link Soviet Archives Exhibit.

The page cannot be found!

This has been a negative example so far. But one thing to be aware of about the Internet is that not everything works all the time. In this case, the reason that search broke down is illuminating. Notice that the entry you've selected begins with "August 5, 1993." This is a piece of dated information—which means that it may be out of date. In this case, the date was a while ago, so perhaps you should search further down the list to see if you can find another reference to the Soviet Archives.

Go back to the previous page by clicking the Back button.

The results of the search on "soviet" reappear.

Find the following text further down the page.

> **North Carolina**: <u>UNC Chapel Hill</u>
>   Includes US Politics, Sun Freeware, Multimedia. You should have a look at the <u>EXPO</u>, including 4 multimedia exhibits: <u>Vatican</u>, <u>Soviet Archive</u>, <u>1492</u>, <u>Dead Sea Scrolls</u>. (<u>cvl</u>)

Follow the link Soviet Archive.

The Soviet Archives page, similar to the one shown in Figure 8.11, is displayed.

The archives are an exciting find. They are an online exhibit—a series of electronically reproduced images of documents available from the Library of

FIGURE 8.11

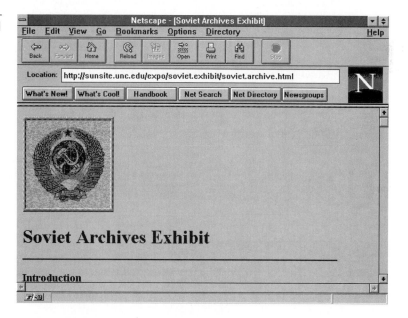

Congress. It provides a unique opportunity, the opportunity to study actual primary source documents from across the network, from anywhere in the world.

For your purposes, this source can be very useful. Although relatively few of the documents actually reflect the time period you seek, a few items deal with the time period surrounding the Russian revolution. As the introductory text tells us, ". . . the documents that the Library of Congress has here chosen from the 500 made available from the Russian archives cover the entire range of Soviet history from the October Revolution of 1917 to the failed coup of August 1991." Conveniently, as well, translations of the documents are provided along with the graphic facsimiles of the originals.

Now that we've found this document, it would be handy to be able to find it again without going through all this work. Netscape offers something called *bookmarks*, which allow you to keep track of sites you've visited so that you can reconnect to them quickly. Let's add this to your bookmarks.

 From the <u>B</u>ookmarks menu, select <u>A</u>dd Bookmark or press (CTRL)-**A**.

The item has been added to the list of bookmarks. Let's check and see.

 Open the <u>B</u>ookmarks menu.

The item you just added appears on the Bookmarks menu, as shown in Figure 8.12.

NOTE: If you need to edit your Bookmark List, select View <u>B</u>ookmarks from the <u>B</u>ookmarks menu, then click on the Edit>> button in the lower portion of this dialog box. The dialog box expands to show more options, as shown in Figure 8.13.

Bookmarks are a useful tool for keeping track of interesting resources you find when exploring the Internet. But enough about bookmarks—let's get on to the task at hand.

 Close the Bookmark List by clicking on the Close button.
Find the following text.

> Please enter the exhibit, by following the golden footsteps on the floor leading into the <u>entrance hall.</u>

FIGURE 8.12

<u>A</u>dd Bookmark	Ctrl+A
View <u>B</u>ookmarks...	Ctrl+B
Soviet Archives Exhibit	

FIGURE 8.13

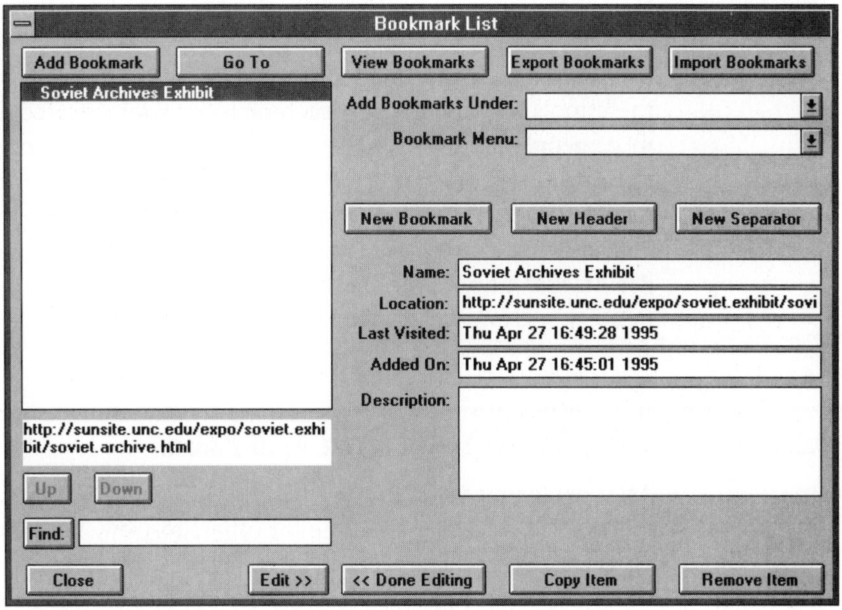

Bookmark List

| Add Bookmark | Go To | | View Bookmarks | Export Bookmarks | Import Bookmarks |

Soviet Archives Exhibit

Add Bookmarks Under: [   ] ▲▼

Bookmark Menu: [   ] ▲▼

| New Bookmark | New Header | New Separator |

Name: Soviet Archives Exhibit

Location: http://sunsite.unc.edu/expo/soviet.exhibit/sovi

Last Visited: Thu Apr 27 16:49:28 1995

Added On: Thu Apr 27 16:45:01 1995

Description:

http://sunsite.unc.edu/expo/soviet.exhibit/soviet.archive.html

| Up | Down |

Find: [   ]

| Close | Edit >> | << Done Editing | Copy Item | Remove Item |

Select entrance hall.

The entrance hall to the Soviet Archives Exhibit is displayed.

You'll find, upon exploring this exhibit, that it is organized as a guided tour—you should be able, by now, to explore it on your own, and find information dealing with the Russian Revolution and the events afterward!

When you are finished exploring, select E_xit from the _File menu to exit Netscape.

THE FUTURE

When we wrote in our UNIX edition of this book, "As this is being written, the Web is growing at an explosive rate," we didn't realize how right we would be about the popularity of the World Wide Web. More tools to browse the Web have appeared, including Netscape, which represents one of the first commercially developed products for the Internet. More services have appeared, including ones from companies, instead of from volunteers. And new standard bodies such as the World Wide Web Consortium (http://www.w3.org/) have emerged to help ensure that the Web continues to evolve in an exciting and dynamic fashion.

What will happen with the World Wide Web, with the Internet, and with any of the tools you have read about here is anybody's guess. But our guess is that these tools will continue to become more sophisticated and more powerful, as more people discover what a valuable resource the Internet is. With the addition of this online community, and as more companies begin to develop new tools for information discovery on the Internet, the resources available to you from your desktop will become rich beyond your wildest imaginings. A computer by itself is just a box, after all. But a computer connected to another computer—a network—is another whole universe for you to explore.

BOX 8.5	**COMPOSING YOUR OWN WEB PAGE**

After exploring the Web for a while, you may want to place your own information and documents online for others to view. The way you can do this is to create documents in HTML—the HyperText Mark-up Language.

HTML is easy to learn. You can be off and running in less than an hour. HTML documents are just like regular text documents, except that special elements are inserted to indicate information about parts of a document. An element is indicated by two tags: one which starts the element (for example, <H1>), and one which ends the element (</H1>). In between those tags, you put text and other information. Some example tags are:

<H1></H1>	Header, Level 1. This indicates a section heading in your document. There are six levels of headers in all.
<P>	Paragragh break. Indicates a break between two paragraphs of text.
<HR>	Horizontal rule. Creates a horizontal divider line to create a visual break between sections of your document.
<IMG SRC="image.gif">	Image. Allows you to include images in your document.
<A HREF="http://some.url.here/"></A>	Anchor. Allows you to make a link to other documents—the magic which makes hypertext work!

Continued on next page

BOX 8.5

COMPOSING YOUR OWN WEB PAGE (*continued*)

A sample HTML document might look like:

```
<HTML>
<HEAD>
<TITLE>This is the document's title.</TITLE>
</HEAD>
<BODY>
<H1>This is a header, level 1.</H1>


This is the first paragraph of my document.<P>


This is another paragraph. Since there is a horizontal rule tag immediately following this paragraph, I
won't put another paragraph break tag after it. Whee!


<HR>


Last modified: February 1, 1995, by <A HREF="http://www.willamette.edu/~jtilton/">Eric Tilton</A>


</BODY>
</HTML>
```

Once you have created your document, you need to place it online, using a
World Wide Web server. You'll need to contact your local computing support
staff to find out if a Web server is already available for use, or if one can be
made available.

Unfortunately, there is not enough space here to give you a thorough introduction to authoring your own hypertext. However, the following two pointers to online resources will help you get started.

◆ http://www.ncsa.uiuc.edu/General/Internet/WWW/HTMLPrimer.html

A Beginner's Guide to HTML—an excellent online tutorial produced by
NCSA, the creators of Mosaic.

◆ http://www.es.cmn.edu/rtilt/cgh/

Composing Good HTML—a guide to help you avoid the common mistakes
made by beginning HTML authors.

SUMMARY

In this chapter, many of the terms and concepts that are necessary to use the Web are introduced:

✦ WWW is a hypertext-based navigation tool for the Internet.

✦ A hypertext document is a document that contains links to other documents and resources.

✦ Links within a document are identified by an underline. You can select and follow the link by clicking on it once. You can navigate back and forth through links by using the button bar.

✦ You can display a WWW page directly by specifying the Uniform Resource Locator (URL) name from the File menu.

✦ You can locate specific text in a WWW document by using the Find command in the Edit menu.

✦ The Internet Search and the Internet Directory pages in Netscape provide access to search engines and directory listings for the WWW.

KEY TERMS

browser	hypertext	server
client	keywords	Uniform Resource
home page	links	Locator (URL)
Hypertext Mark-up Language (HTML)	page	Web

REVIEW QUESTIONS

1. What is the difference between WWW and Gopher?

2. What is the purpose of HyperText Mark-up Language?

3. What is a hypertext document?

4. Why do you have to know the Uniform Resource Locator name?

5. In Netscape, how do you recognize, select, and follow a link?

6. In Netscape, how do you find a particular text within WWW?

7. In Netscape, how do you scroll through a page in WWW?

8. How do you start a subject-oriented search in WWW?

9. How do you start an index-oriented search in WWW?

10. Once you locate a document in WWW, what can you do with it?

EXERCISES

1. Find out what a euphonium is and how it differs from a baritone.

2. What does the White Rabbit say to Alice at the beginning of *Alice in Wonderland*?

3. When did the Vandals of Africa occupy the coastal cities of Sardinia?

4. Some of you may soon be facing decisions about which graduate or under-graduate institutions to attend. Find a WWW resource that can help in making this decision. (Online information supplied by the institutions themselves would be good for this.)

DISCUSSION TOPICS

1. What kinds of advantages does the World Wide Web have over a tool such as Gopher or FTP? What kinds of disadvantages? What might be a situation in which you would want to use the Web over another tool?

2. The resources available in a library can often be trusted as authoritative. One thing that is problematic about online resources is that it is much more difficult to determine how valid the resources are. Discuss reasons why this might be.

3. Explore the Russia and Eastern Europe area of the Virtual Library (refer to the section Subject-Oriented Catalogs of Information if you don't remember how to locate the Virtual Library). Is this more or less useful than other sources? Does it say anything different?

PROJECTS

1. THE SITUATION:

I sent a friend of mine an (English) quote from a German World Wide Web server which touted how cool German is for discussing philosophy. She responded with "Nicht schlecht, aber wo ist die 'Est-set' auf diesen Amerianische Tastatur? Mann kann nicht philosophische sprechen mit kein Schwnaz auf der 'B'!" I don't even speak German! Is there anything on the Internet that can help me translate this?

YOUR PROJECT: Translate the German response into English with assistance from resources on the Internet. List resources you used, along with their locations (or search paths).

STRATEGIES: Check the Gopher and Web subject trees under "language." Be sure to search indexes like Veronica and the W3 catalog for "German." Don't forget how useful a FAQ can be!

2. THE SITUATION:

I'm researching the decisions of the Supreme Court during the Bush Administration through as much of the Clinton Administration as possible.

YOUR PROJECT: Find and list resources you can locate pertaining to the Supreme Court. What is the oldest information you can get? List resources along with their location or search path. Also, give samples of your findings.

STRATEGIES: Check in subject trees under areas such as "law" and "government publications." Look for forums and active discussions of legal issues and the courts.

3. THE SITUATION:

I've been assigned to give a presentation about Dante Alighieri, author of *The Divine Comedy,* and his contemporary critics. I need to find out about his contemporaries.

YOUR PROJECT: Find resources that will be of assistance. List the location or the search path. Also, give samples of your findings.

STRATEGIES: Look for collections of literature resources in Gopher and on the Web. FAQs and members of electronic forums may be able to point you toward resources.

4. THE SITUATION:

I'm going to be traveling abroad to Lesotho in a month, and I'd like to bone up on the culture, the history, and so on.

YOUR PROJECT: Find sources of information on this country. Are any of these sources current or updated frequently? List resources found, along with location or search path. Give samples of your findings.

STRATEGIES: Government agencies concerned with foreign relations and the status of foreign countries, as well as international organizations, may have information available about various aspects of different countries.

5. THE SITUATION:

I've got an Italian Renaissance Art History class this semester.

YOUR PROJECT: Find images of art, any scholarly forums, and any other non-image materials for the discussion of Renaissance art. What other art genres can you find? List resources found along with the locations.

STRATEGIES: Check Gopher and Web indexes for words relating to art, the Renaissance, or well-known artists and artisans of the time. Scholarly forums and their FAQs may be able to put you on the right track.

6. THE SITUATION:

I would like to send letters to my national representatives in government. I'd like to know whether I can send them e-mail, and what would be done with the e-mail I would send to them. If I can't contact them by e-mail, I need their postal addresses and fax numbers.

YOUR PROJECT: Find out whether and how one can send e-mail to one's national representatives. If you can't send e-mail, what other ways can you contact them? What kind of reception do you get by e-mail?

STRATEGIES: Government information servers are appearing. Those servers run by agencies or bodies with whom your representatives are affiliated may give you addresses or phone numbers. It is not unheard of for different political figures to make a show of network information access on their own, unconnected to the government itself.

7. THE SITUATION:

I know that the National Science Foundation provides information on available science grants, and guidelines and specifications for writing grants. I'd like to see if there is anything available for me to apply for; I'm an undergraduate student in organic chemistry.

YOUR PROJECT: Find the resources. List them along with location or search path. Give samples of your findings.

STRATEGIES: Science forums on the Internet will surely be able to point you to the NSF access points. Searching with Veronica or the Web indexes should move you in that direction rapidly as well.

8. THE SITUATION:

I use a UNIX computer, and I'd like to find some clear help and tutorials on using UNIX. Are there any sources for this on the Internet?

YOUR PROJECT: Locate a UNIX tutorial on the Internet. List location or search path.

STRATEGIES: Newsgroups about various aspects of UNIX should, through other readers or FAQs, be able to point you towards what is available. Archie, Veronica, and Web indexes should turn up material as well.

9. THE SITUATION:

Being an astronomy major, I am interested in the goings-on at NASA. Is there any way that I can get up-to-date information about NASA missions or projects through the Internet?

YOUR PROJECT: Locate resources and list location or search path. Give samples of your findings.

STRATEGIES: Government agencies like NASA have been on the Internet for quite some time, in a variety of different formats. Searching for the names of different NASA agencies or missions, as well as the names of different observatories, will turn up information and servers.

10. THE SITUATION:

I'm graduating soon, and I'd like to know if there are any ways to both find out about job opportunities and advertise myself to prospective employers.

YOUR PROJECT: Locate resources on the Internet. List location or search path. Give samples of your findings.

STRATEGIES: When looking for a job outside the Internet, one looks at newspapers and newsletters, employment agencies, and at individual companies and organizations in which employment is desired. What similar sources are there on the Internet to peruse?

INTERNET RESOURCES AND DIRECTORIES

The Internet provides considerable help and information about itself; how well one makes use of them depends on one's basic working knowledge of the tools. Collected here are some of the more important Internet resources. These include pointers to collected resources, listings of collected resources, and other tidbits that you may find useful in your wanderings of the 'net. Because printed lists of resources are usually out of date, it is often best to use the Internet itself to retrieve lists of resources currently available. These resources are intended to supplement those covered in the chapters of this book.

GENERAL RESOURCES

Yanoff's Special Internet Connections

This is a compilation of interesting and useful subject-specific resources and sites compiled by Scott Yanoff. It is updated twice monthly and is available in a number of ways:

newsgroup	alt.internet.services (published the first and fifteenth of each month)
ftp to	csd4.csd.uwm.edu, look in /pub/inet.services.txt
Gopher to	gopher.csd.uwm.edu, look in Remote Information Services
WWW to	http://www.uwm.edu/Mirror/inet.services.html

John December's List: "Information Sources: the Internet and Computer-Mediated Communication"

A rich WWW resource containing information on many topics. Of particular note is the section on Internet guides and help. This is a good place to find out what sorts of information about using the Internet are available on the Internet.

http://www.rpi.edu/Internet/Guides/decemj/icmc/toc3/html

net-happenings

This is an excellent announcements listserv for Internet occurrences and re-sources of all kinds, run by Gleason Sackman. It is rather high traffic, so be pre-pared for a flood of various tidbits!

Send mail to	net-happenings-request@is.internic.net
with the message	subscribe *\<your name\>*

The Internic Scout Report

A weekly publication containing information on what's new and interesting in the world of the Internet. Published by the InterNIC.

http://www.internic.net/inforguide.html
gopher://gopher.is.internic.net:70/11/infoguide/scout-report

E-MAIL RESOURCES

Yanoff's Inter-network Mail Guide

For more extensive information on mailing to and from many different net-works around the world, refer to this guide for starters. Updated periodically.

ftp to	csd4.csd.uwm.edu
look in	/pub/internetwork-mail-guide

USENET RESOURCES

*.answers newsgroups

These are the designated general information newsgroups for each of the major newsgroup hierarchies (alt, sci, mist, talk, rec, etc.). You can check these news-groups for information and periodic postings of the FAQs for the newsgroups in those hierarchies.

alt.internet.services

This is a newsgroup devoted to questions and answers about any resource on the Internet, but *not* about specific tools and programs, or new-user questions. If you have a question about how to access a particular site, or changes with particular resources, and cannot find an answer anywhere else, then post to the group.

Newsgroup FAQs

Extensive collections of newsgroup FAQs exist. These FAQs are principally archived at one site.

ftp to	rtfm.mit.edu
look in	/pub/usenet/

The FAQs in the rtfm archive can also be accessed by sending commands to the rtfm ftp-mail server. To get instructions for requesting files, send a message to:

mail-server@rtfm.MIT.EDU

with the message body:

help

There are various mirrors of this archive around the world. The following lists various FTP sites you can access, along with the directory in which the information is located. Please exhaust those geographically nearest to your site before trying archives further away.

ftp.uu.net	/usenet/

In Europe:

cc1.kuleuven.ac.be	/anonymous.202/
cnam.cnam.fr	/pub/FAQ
grasp1.univ-lyon1.fr	/pub/faq/
ftp.cs.ruu.nl	/pub/NEWS.ANSWERS
ftp.win.tue.nl	/pub/usenet/news.answers

In Taiwan:

nctuccca.edu.tw	/USENET/FAQ/

GOPHER RESOURCES

Information about Gopher, Gopher clients, servers, and utilities can be found at the University of Minnesota Gopher.

Gopher to   gopher.tc.umn.edu.

The Clearinghouse of Subject-Oriented Internet Resource Guides

This is a collection of subject guides to resources on the Internet written by students in the Master of Library Science program at the University of Michigan. The Clearinghouse also lists many other useful subject guides.

Gopher to   una.hh.lib.umich.edu.

U.S. Government Gopher Servers

Gopher to   stis.nsf.gov
look in   Other U.S. Government Gopher Servers

WORLD WIDE WEB RESOURCES

World Wide Web Overview

Document leading to descriptions and technical details of the Web as well as to resources and collections of resources, including many listed here. Use a Web client to connect to:

> http://info.cern.ch/hypertext/WWW/LineMode/Defaults/default.html

Internet Resources Meta-Index

A loosely organized categorization of Internet resources. Use a Web client to connect to:

> http://www.ncsa.uiuc.edu/SDG/Software/Mosaic/MetaIndex.html

Searchable Catalog of Web Resources

A search engine that searches "known" WWW sites by keyword. Use a Web client to connect to:

> http://cui_www.unige.ch/w3catalog

What's New with the World Wide Web

A series of pages updated daily with any new developments or servers announced on the Web. Use a Web client to connect to:

> http://www.ncsa.uiuc.edu/SDG/Software/Mosaic/Docs/whats-new.html

World Wide Web Sites by Geography

Leads to both an interactive map or directories by area of servers around the world. Use a Web client to connect to:

> http://wings.buffalo.edu/world

Also of note at this site are the "Best of the Web" awards, located at:

> http://wings.buffalo.edu/contest/

The WWW Virtual Library: Subject Catalogue

> http://info.cern.ch/hypertext/DataSources/BySubject/Overview.html

The Yahoo Directory

> http://www.yahoo.com/

In particular, you can locate all the Web browsers in:

> http://www.yahoo.com/Computers/World_Wide_Web/Browsers/

WAIS RESOURCES

Additional Gopher servers that allow access to WAIS:

ftp.sprintlink.net
info.mcc.ac.uk

Hints and Warnings about Using "WAIS" Software for Searching

By Ernest Perez, this is a concise discussion of getting the most out of WAIS searching. It is available via Gopher at:

gopher.willamette.edu

FURTHER READING

TECHNICALLY ORIENTED BOOKS

Stevens, W. Richard. *TCP/IP Illustrated*. Reading, Mass: Addison-Wesley Publishing Company, 1994.

Tanenbaum, Andrew S. *Computer Networks*. Englewood Cliffs, NJ: Prentice Hall, 1988.

Todino, Grace and John Strang. *Learning the UNIX Operating System*. Newton, MA: O'Reilly & Associates, Inc., 1993.

GETTING CONNECTED

Engle, Mary, et al. *Internet Connections: A Librarian's Guide to Dial-Up Access and Use*. Lita Monographs 3. Chicago: Library and Information Technology Association, 1993.

Estrada, Susan. *Connecting to the Internet: An O'Reilly Buyer's Guide*. Sebastapol, CA: O'Reilly & Associates, Inc., 1993.

Marine, April, et al. *Internet: Getting Started*. Englewood Cliffs, NJ: PTR Prentice Hall, 1992.

Peal, David. *Access the Internet!*, San Francisco: SYBEX, 1994.

GENERAL USE BOOKS

The following lists books written for the novice Internet user. Several excellent guides also exist on the Internet itself. Refer to the chapters on Gopher and FTP to learn how to find and retrieve those documents. Also, see *John December's List* listed in the Internet Resources and Directories section.

Dern, Daniel. *The Internet Guide for New Users*. New York: McGraw-Hill, 1994.

Engst, Adam C. *Internet Starter Kit for Macintosh*. 2nd ed. Indianapolis: Hayden Books, 1994.

Fisher, Sharon. *Riding the Internet Highway*. Carmel, IN: New Riders, 1994.

Gilster, Paul. *The Internet Navigator*. 2nd ed. New York: Wiley, 1994.

Glossbrenner, Alfred. *Internet 101: A College Student's Guide.* New York: Windcrest/McGraw-Hill, 1994.

Hahn, Harley. *Internet: The Complete Reference*. New York: Osborne McGraw-Hill, 1994.

Henderson, Harry. *The Waite Group's Internet How-To*. Corte Madera, CA: Waite Group Press, 1994.

Kehoe, Brendan P. *Zen and the Art of the Internet: A Beginner's Guide*. 3rd ed. Englewood Cliffs, NJ: PTR Prentice Hall, 1994.

Kochmer, Jonathan. *The Internet Passport: NorthWestNet's Guide to Our Online World*. 4th ed. Bellevue, WA: NorthWestNet, 1994.

Krol, Ed. *The Whole Internet: User's Guide & Catalog.* 2nd ed. Sebastopol, CA: O'Reilly & Associates, Inc., 1994.

LaQuey, Tracy L. *The Internet Companion: A Beginner's Guide to Global Networking*. 2nd ed. Reading, Mass.: Addison-Wesley Pub. Co., 1994.

Levine, John R. and Carol Baroudi. *The Internet for Dummies*. 2nd ed. San Mateo, CA: IDG Books, 1994.

Smith, Richard and Mark Gibbs. *Navigating the Internet*. Indianapolis: SAMS Publishing, 1994.

Tennant, Roy, et al. *Crossing the Internet Threshold: An Instructional Handbook*. Berkeley, CA: Library Solutions Press, 1993.

Veljkou, Mark D. *Pocket Guide to the Internet*. Westport: Meckler, 1994.

BOOKS FOR CITING ELECTRONIC RESOURCES IN SCHOLARLY PAPERS

The Chicago Manual of Style. 14th ed. Chicago: University of Chicago Press, 1993.

This standard work now includes information on how to cite information retrieved electronically.

Li, Xia and Nancy Crane. *Electronic Style: A Guide to Citing Electronic Information.* Westport: Meckler, 1993.

This book is devoted entirely to how to cite online resources. Includes many useful examples.

GLOSSARY

address   Each machine on the Internet has a unique address (*see* IP address). Each user on a machine has his or her own unique address, usually comprised of a username and domain name, separated by an at (@) sign. For example, a person with the username portofon on the machine at Willamette University with the domain name willamette.edu has the address portofon@willamette.edu.

adjacency   A index search operator, "adj," that lets you specify that the first keyword be adjacent to the second keyword. For example, "new adj mexico" means you want the word "new" to appear next to the word "mexico."

anonymous FTP   FTP (File Transfer Protocol) is a computer program that allows users to transfer files between machines on the Internet. Anonymous FTP allows user access to remote machines with the login name of "anonymous" for the purpose of transferring publicly accessible files.

Archie   Supposedly short for "Archive," Archie is a program that maintains a database of files on the Internet that are accessible via anonymous FTP.

articles   In Usenet News, individual messages are often referred to as postings or articles.

ASCII file   The American Standard Code for Information Interchange (ASCII) is a standard for representing text in a machine. Many machines can understand ASCII coded files, whereas they might not understand files that were coded by programs such as word processors or spreadsheets, although most programs usually have an option to save files in ASCII format. ASCII files are sometimes referred to as *text files* or *plain text files*.

BITNET   The "Because It's Time NETwork" is an e-mail and file-sharing network used by a large number of academic and research institutions. There are many mail gateways between the Internet and BITNET.

bookmarks   A feature found in Gopher and Netscape that lets you keep track of a site or Web page you found useful or interesting.

Boolean operators   A method of searching for information, often used in databases and online library catalogs, using the Boolean operators AND, OR, and NOT.

browser   A client for WWW.

browsing   A method of finding material in any of the various Internet services, by which you make a selection and see what options are displayed. Although it may not appear to be very sophisticated, it is often surprisingly effective, especially when few other search methods are available.

Campus Wide Information Systems (CWIS)   A software system for electronically providing information of interest to the members of a particular community, most frequently a college or university. An increasing number of CWISs are developed using Gopher.

client   A computer or process that relies on the resources of another computer or process (server). The client for WWW is called a browser.

client/server model   The software configuration in which there are two parts to the program—the server, which holds data, and clients, which query and retrieve data from the server. Client and server can reside on the same or distant machines.

compressed files   Files that have been compacted to allow for faster transfer or distribution. These files need to be uncompressed before they can be used.

CSO server   A searchable index, usually found on a Gopher, that provides information about users at the particular site.

domain name   The Internet convention of constructing a name for a computer on the Internet. Domain names were created for human use (substituting for numeric IP addresses, which can be confusing).

electronic conference (e-conference)   E-conferences are electronic discussions on particular topics, conducted by groups of interested users. E-mail listservs and Usenet News are often used for e-conferencing.

electronic journal (e-journal)   Periodicals that are distributed electronically. Listservs, Usenet News, and World Wide Web are often used for distribution.

electronic mail (e-mail)   Messages sent via electronic networks. Many networks support this capability. The user must have access to electronic mail software in order to read and send e-mail.

electronic newsletter (e-newsletter)   See electronic journal (e-journal).

File Transfer Protocol (FTP)   A protocol that allows a machine on the Internet to receive or send files to another machine.

flame war   A Usenet phenomenon in which two or more people post messages that are intentionally inflammatory, derogatory, or argumentative.

Frequently Asked Questions (FAQ)   Pronounced *fack*, a list of often-asked questions and answers about a particular subject or area of knowledge. A FAQ is usually posted to a Usenet newsgroup to keep people from asking the same questions over and over again.

Full Group List   A list of all available newsgroups.

full-privilege FTP   Using File Transfer Protocol (FTP) to send or receive files on a machine for which you have an account, rather than using FTP anonymously. The user has direct access to his or her files. *See also* anonymous FTP and File Transfer Protocol.

global list   The list of all listserv lists on BITNET. You can search the global list for a topic and discover the names of lists covering that topic.

Gopher   A document delivery system for retrieving information from the Internet. The information is stored on Gopher servers and retrieved by Gopher clients. The name Gopher comes from the mascot of the University of Minnesota, where the program was developed.

Gopher client   Software providing a user interface to the Gopher document delivery system. A Gopher client will allow you to browse through the many Gopher servers seamlessly.

Gopher server   Software run on host computers that provides information for Gopher.

GopherSpace   Everything and anything which is available from all the Gopher servers on the Internet—this is a lot of information. Usage examples: "I found it in GopherSpace!" or "Search GopherSpace for it."

Group window   A window that shows all newsgroups to which you are subscribed.

hierarchical file structure   A method of storing files in directories and subdirectories in a hierarchical fashion. The hierarchical structure can be conceptualized as a tree, with a trunk (directory), branches from the trunk (subdirectories), and branches from branches. The leaves at the end of the branches are the files themselves.

home page   The document where a World Wide Web browser starts. The home page will usually contain references to documents of common interest. Browsers allow the user to get to the home page of any WWW document.

hostname   The portion of the domain name that refers to the host itself. For example, in the domain name jupiter.willamette.edu, jupiter is the hostname within the willamette.edu domain.

hypertext   More than just plain text. A document that contains links to other documents and allows the user to move easily from one related document to another. A hypertext book might have sections linked with excerpts from another book.

Hypertext Mark-up Language (HTML)   The hypertext document format used by the World Wide Web.

Hytelnet   Peter Scott's database of publicly accessible Internet sites. Hytelnet includes libraries; Campus Wide Information Systems (CWIS); Gopher, WAIS, and WWW systems; Freenets and more.

index   A WAIS index takes a large body of information (usually in the form of multiple documents) and creates a database of words that can be searched. When an index search is performed, the documents containing the keywords specified can be retrieved by the user.

Internet Protocol (IP) address   A numeric address in the format www.xxx.yyy.zzz that is assigned to a machine on a TCP/IP network. IP addresses are unique and refer to a specific machine on the Internet. An example address would be 158.104.1.1. The periods are read as "dot." *See also* domain name.

keyword   A word that is relevant to the information being sought.

links   A link is the information that a client program (such as Gopher or Netscape) uses to get a resource from a server program. The link has all the information necessary for the client program to contact the correct server and request the desired information.

list processor   One of several names for a program that sends e-mail to and from a particular list of subscribers. *See* listserv.

listserv   The original BITNET program used to send e-mail to and from a particular list of subscribers. Listservs, and the various similar programs (list processor, mail reflector, mailing list), are usually organized around some broad or narrow topic that subscribers discuss.

logout   The process of disconnecting from a computer system.

mail reflector   One of several names for a program that sends e-mail to and from a particular list of subscribers. *See* listserv.

mailing list   One of several names for a program that sends e-mail to and from a particular list of subscribers. *See* listserv.

moderated list   A listserv or newsgroup that is moderated, in that postings are reviewed by a moderator (usually the list owner) before being forwarded to the entire forum, if at all.

moderator   One of several names for a program that sends e-mail to and from a particular list of subscribers. *See* listserv.

natural language   Language that you use in everyday life as opposed to languages that require special terms such as Boolean operators.

Netfind   Given a last name and the name of an organization, Netfind will search for that organization's computers and any names matching on those computers.

netnews   *See* news.

news   Officially known as Usenet, also known as newsgroups, a collection of thousands of topically organized electronic forums called newsgroups. *See* Usenet and newsgroups.

news administrator   The person at an Internet site who is responsible for the maintenance of the news programs and newsfeed.

newsfeed   The newsfeed is the source (generally another Internet host) for news articles and groups.

newsgroups   The individual electronic forums that are part of Usenet. An individual newsgroup will often (attempt to) have a fairly narrow and

defined subject area demonstrated by its name; for example, rec.arts.brewery and sci.botany.

page   A screen on the Wide World Web.

phone book   A database of persons at a particular site, listing whatever information (e-mail addresses, phone numbers, positions) that seems relevant.

plain text file   *See* ASCII file.

platform   A particular variety of computer, with different features, capabilities and drawbacks from other platforms. Macintosh, Windows, and UNIX are examples of different platforms.

POP mail   A mail program that works with a POP server. The mail is sent to the POP server and is accessed through a computer running a POP client software. When you run the client, the mail is transferred from the server to the machine running the client.

POP mail server   Usually installed on a centralized computer system, the server receives mail to be distributed to POP clients.

port   The communication channel on a computer that one Internet program uses to communicate with another. A gopher client hails a gopher server on a specific port, commonly number 70.

post, postings   An article or message sent to a newsgroup or listserv, reminiscent of posting a bill or leaflet on a bulletin board or other such public physical information forum.

relevance feedback   A feature on WAIS that lets you ask for more documents that are similar to the ones already found.

root gopher   The first menu that appears when you start a Gopher client program. This is the point from which you start accessing all other Gopher selections.

router A device on the network that moves packets from one network to another.

server The distribution side of the client/server model. A server is a program that holds information, providing it to clients on request.

subject tree A Gopher server having a menu organized by general subject heading, similar to a library.

subscribe To sign up to receive information. On the Internet, you can subscribe to newsgroups and electronic mailing lists.

TCP/IP (Transfer Control Protocol/Internet Protocol) A major protocol used over the Internet to provide reliable, ordered, end-to-end transmission of information. The Internet Protocol allows information to be transferred across the Internet, and the Transfer Control Protocol ensures that the information arrives in the correct order.

Telnet The standard program for logging onto computers on the Internet.

terminal emulation A process by which a computer acts like a specific kind of terminal when connected to another computer. This is necessary because, before the advent of personal computers, many people accessed computers through terminals. These terminals typically had special character sequences which would move the cursor, highlight text, or provide other functions for sophisticated text placement. Programs would use the character sequences when outputting. Later, when personal computers became standard, programs were written to enable personal computers to be used as terminals for accessing other computers. Many emulators mimic the VT100 terminals. The Telnet program is an example of a terminal emulator, and is still used to connect to UNIX machines.

The 'net One of many hip, urban ways to refer to the Internet. Other pundits use "Information Superhighway," "Infobahn," or "The Matrix."

The Internet A collection of networks using TCP/IP protocols to communicate. The uncapitalized form, "an internet," refers to any collection of networks which can intercommunicate.

threaded A collection of Usenet news articles arranged by topic. A thread refers to a thread of conversation, with articles and responses grouped together in order.

top-level domain The most general (rightmost) part of the domain name, usually a two-letter country code specifying the country controlling the domain if outside the United States, or GOV, EDU, COM or MIL for government, educational, commercial, or military sites, respectively, within the United States.

Uniform Resource Locator (URL) A machine and (some claim) human-readable standard for locating resources on the Internet. A URL describes the scheme for retrieving the information, the Internet host on which the information is located, and the location of the information on that host.

UNIX An operating system developed in the 1970s at Bell Labs, and now one of the most popular operating systems for multiple-user computers. It is also one of the most common operating systems on the Internet. The name puns "Multics," an operating system developed at the same time by Bell Labs.

unsubscribe To take your name off a list for receiving information. On the Internet, you can unsubscribe to newsgroups and electronic mailing lists.

Usenet A collection of thousands of topically named newsgroups, the computers that exchange some or all of these newsgroups, and the community of people who read or submit Usenet news. Not all Internet hosts subscribe to Usenet newsgroups, and Usenet newsgroups may be received by non-Internet hosts.

username   A unique identifier for a user. The name by which one has authorized access to a computer system, and the part of an Internet address by which a person or service is known in an Internet address.

Veronica   A searchable index of items available via Gopher. The name is an acronym for "Very Easy Rodent Oriented Net-wide Index to Computerized Archives."

Web   Short for "World Wide Web."

Wide Area Information Server (WAIS)   WAIS is a method for creating full text indexes of information, then serving that information over the Internet. WAIS is the most popular way of indexing information on the Internet. WAIS-specific clients are available, but WAIS indexes can also be accessed via Gopher and the World Wide Web.

World Wide Web (WWW)   A method for providing distributed information on the Internet. In the World Wide Web, documents are hypertext, which means that they can provide links to other documents. With the advent of multimedia browsing tools such as Netscape, many people believe the future of the Internet will be here.

INDEX